ASTONISHING SCOTLAND!

A Cheeky Thesaurus of

SCOTTISHNESS

JIM HEWITSON

'To have common glories in the past, a common will in the present; to
have accomplished great things together, to wish to do so again, that
is the essential condition for being a nation.'
Ernest Renan, 1882

Black & White Publishing

Also by Jim Hewitson

Clinging to the Edge: Journals from an Orkney Island
Far Off in Sunlit Places: Scots in Australia/New Zealand
Rebecca the Racoon
Scotching the Myths
Tam Blake & Co.: Scots in America

First published in 2003
by Black & White Publishing Ltd
99 Giles Street, Edinburgh EH6 6BZ

ISBN 1 902927 67 2

A CIP catalogue record for this book is available
from The British Library.

Cover illustration by Bob Dewar
Printed and bound by Creative Print and Design

CONTENTS

INTRODUCTION

For centuries, the only history that was worth a toss seemed to deal with great and weighty political, constitutional and legal matters. For the most part this was English history, and the only time the Scots, Welsh or Irish appeared on the scene was when they were hindering the smooth operation of the English system. It is only in the past half-century that Scottish history, and in particular Scottish social history – the story of the way people lived – have become important areas of study. As Scotland, with its own parliament again, edges nervously into a new era, fascinating pathways along which we can explore the story of our nation have been opening up.

In this book I make an idiosyncratic sortie into some of the more 'off the wall' aspects of Scotland's story. For me, one really comforting thing about this batch of yarns is that our Scottish ancestors seem to have been just as daft as we are. More than anything, I hope this modest wee collection inspires you to read more about Scottish history, heritage, folklore and myth. There is plenty now out there.

Scots, to paraphrase someone much wiser than myself, are the product and embodiment of their own past. I hope that, by the time you've skimmed *Astonishing Scotland*, you'll see just what a complex beastie you are. And if you get as much fun out of dipping into this collection of off-cuts from the story of Scotland as I have had in harvesting and putting my own spin on them, then my labours will not have been in vain. As one of my Aberdeen tutors is wont to say, 'Everything okay so far?' (Apologies, Derrick.) If so, let us proceed.

Jim Hewitson
Inverurie, April 2003

CHAPTER 1

Away an' Tie Up yer Heid!

Tales that Take Some Swallowing

The Hammer and the Harpy

There are two interesting – and conflicting – theories why Edward I of England (1239–1307) received his nickname 'Hammer of the Scots'. One school of thought suggests that it was acquired because of the manner in which he battered the Scots into submission, while alternatively it is argued, more prosaically, that through his oppressive attempts at over-lordship he forged and hammered Scotland into a nation.

In an eerie echo of this latter theory, there are Scots who believe that, without the almost medieval contempt for Scotland displayed by Conservative Prime Minister Margaret Thatcher in the 1980s and 1990s, we would never have worked up a sufficient head of steam to campaign – successfully, as we now know – for our own Parliament. Perhaps we should erect a statue to the Iron Lady in Parliament Square? Edward may have been reviled by the Scottish nation for his dirty deeds, but his status as an anointed king still saw him being sought out by hundreds of Scots anxious to be 'touched' for scrofula, a skin disease also known as 'The King's Evil', which it was thought could only be cured by a laying-on of hands by a legitimate monarch.

Nothing Like a Hard Tying-up

In 1650, Scotland was blighted by the 'Irish ague' – a 'terrible sair pain' in the cranium – which was blamed, as usual, on the Highlanders/Gaels/Barbarians and which was cured, apparently, by a 'hard tying-up of the head'. Give me a painkiller or a tight bunnet any day. A century earlier a disease raged in Edinburgh which was mysteriously called 'The New Acquaintance', characterised by coughing and a sair heid. The court did not escape, and even Queen Mary was said to be one degree under. It is now thought that the illness was our auld acquaintance – influenza.

Gone Today, Hair Tomorrow

If you thought anxiety over baldness was a symptom of the self-conscious, over-stressed twenty-first century, then think again. Over the years all sorts of bizarre remedies for baldness have been tried. One of the most popular in seventeenth-century Edinburgh was the application of the burnt ashes of dove's dung. Elsewhere, burying mice in a pot by the fire and leaving them for a year before applying the resultant mixture was highly recommended. With this remedy came a serious warning that gloves should always be worn because the mixture would promote the growth of hair even on the fingertips.

Sign of the Times

There was consternation in Orkney post-Christmas 2000 when, included among the items in a January sale, was a nativity scene. It was displayed with a sign spreading the sad tidings, 'Half-price – Baby Jesus Missing'.

Beach Lore

We're justly proud here in Scotland of our silver beaches but, with such a vast, indented coastline, we tend to get more than our share of sea litter, flotsam and jetsam – and not only crisp packets and juice cans. A recent survey revealed that among items found were a purple inflatable dinosaur, a fridge door, a number 49 bingo ball and a plastic pre-decimalisation washing-up bottle. The longevity of this last item is worrying. Scientists tell us that some man-made items in the ocean decay faster than others – a movie ticket takes only two weeks; a woollen sock up to a year; a tin can up to a century and a plastic bottle perhaps 450 years. Does this mean that the plastic fruit-juice container at your feet in the sand might have been around since the Reformation? Scary!

The Bells! The Bells!

When the bells of St Giles in Edinburgh rang out to signal the Union between Scotland and England in 1707, there was a dubious omen for the future which has been cast up by cynical nationalists ever since. The first melody which clanged out across the capital was, 'Why should I be so sad on my wedding day?' A campanologist with attitude, methinks.

Chewing over Scottish History

One of Scotland's most important early historical documents, *The Scotichronicon* – now held at Cambridge University – was written by Walter Bower in the 1400s. But an Archbishop of Canterbury saved it from a lamentable end. When he re-discovered the priceless tome, rats had already begun to make a serious meal of Scotland's story.

The Comforts of Home

Robertson of Struan was given the government commander Sir John Cope's carriage as his share of the booty after the spectacular Jacobite success at Prestonpans in 1745. Among items in the coach were rolls of a substance thought at first to have been a salve to be applied to wounds. It transpired that the rolls were chocolate for the General's evening cuppa. Historians agree that Johnny Cope kept running that day and for him there was no sweet taste of victory.

Scarlet-Kneed Highlanders

When Queen Victoria, during a review of her Highland troops, noted that her soldiers' knees had been scratched by the rough uniform kilts, she ordered that the kilts should in future be woven in softer commercial wool.

The Celtic Connection

Morgan – a distinctively Welsh name – may someday belong to a Scottish clan. The Morgan Society (not the car enthusiasts) is up and running in Scotland and working to establish their Scottish/Celtic roots.

Whaur's the Shop Steward?

The first recorded instance of a Scottish industrial dispute comes in the annals of the medieval monks of Inchcolm Abbey in the River Forth, who downed psalters because of the abusive behaviour of the abbot.

Speculate to Accumulate

Before the Life Assurance Act of 1774, gamblers used to take out insurance policies on the lives of personalities with dangerous lifestyles, in the hope of making a quick killing. One of the most popular targets for speculators keen on a wee flutter was Bonnie Prince Charlie during the '45 uprising. By the time of Culloden, I would guess, premiums must have been impossibly high.

Sticks and Stones

In the nineteenth century, Barnhill Poorhouse in Glasgow's Springburn District demanded that able-bodied inmates make up to 350 bundles of firewood or break up five hundredweight of stone daily for their keep. Failure to meet this target meant a day in solitary on a bread-and-water regime.

Jet-Propelled Prancing

Overfed courtiers breaking wind on the dance floor was a cheeky theme chosen by James IV's court poet William Dunbar for one of his highly respected poems, 'Dance in the Queen's Chalmer'. 'Gavotte are you up to out there?' was the cry from the sidelines.

Not Yer Average Bouncy Castle

A full-scale model of Edinburgh Castle, used in the late 1990s when the capital's annual tattoo visited Wellington, is still in storage in New Zealand.

The Man Had No Soul

'I' pronounced 'Ee' – the Gaelic name for the island of Iona, launchpad for Colum-cille or St Columba's missionary campaigns in the north of Scotland and a highly respected European centre of learning in the pre-Viking era – is one of the shortest, and most mysterious, words in the language. It may mean 'isle' but, equally, it may have some connection with yew trees. By 1859 Iona was fast becoming a popular tourist target with three steamers weekly from Oban. Mind you, one travel writer was distinctly underwhelmed by his visit, finding that the ruins fascinated visitors although the island had no 'natural beauty'.

Difficult News to Swallow

In 1571 government officials were pondering reports that a messenger sent to Jedburgh in the Borders to declare the re-establishment of Queen Mary's rule had been forced to eat his despatches, presumably in addition to the contents of his lunch box.

Heritage up in Smoke

Baptism and marriage records were taken from the parish of Castleton in Roxburghshire in 1649 by Roundheads from Oliver Cromwell's invading army. The soldiers used the priceless genealogical records to light their tobacco pipes.

Patching up Scottish History

Such is the demand from incurable romantics for Jacobite relics that, in the late 1990s, a private collector paid £1,725 for a moth-eaten 6-inch square of plaid said to have been worn by Bonnie Prince Charlie. If you feel disappointed at having missed out on this great opportunity, then don't despair – there are apparently six similar pieces of scabby cloth left around after the Inverness-shire Rout of Moy in 1746. And if you're really stuck I can offer off-cuts from my ancient 'Hunting Hewitson' kilt worn with pride during my service with the 3rd Clydebank scouts and cubs and on campaign in Devon and Isle of Wight. During the Apollo moon missions, US astronauts of Scottish descent got into the habit of carrying patches of tartan on their expeditions. Clans Armstrong, MacBean and Ross were all represented.

Ah'll Jingle Jangle Ye . . .

One of the ancient and odd privileges of the doorkeepers at the Court of Session in Edinburgh is to demand a 5-shilling penalty from any noisy individual who appears in the court precincts wearing spurs. You'll be in even bigger trouble if you attempt to hitch your cuddy to a bollard in Parliament Square. Be warned!

Discipline Run Riot

The Scots liking for a good scrap has often been exported and Scottish mercenaries figure in many of the most important European campaigns. A Scot called Gordon was among a group who slew the awesome Czech Count Wallenstein, who once ordered an officer put to death because his spurs clanked.

Pass the Bunnet

Some homespun medical ideas from the Scottish annals do indeed take some swallowing – for example, if you were having trouble producing male offspring, the advice for the man was to keep his boots (or bunnet!) on during sex. If a baby girl was on the agenda then it was necessary to place an axe under the bed before you got down to business. If your sexual performance was suffering as a result of weak legs, the answer was to climb into the still-warm, disembowelled carcass of a sheep. Obvious when you think about it.

In the seventeenth century, many of these remedies were concerned with the scourge of gout. Some of the more entertaining include the application of the skin of a vulture to the patient's heel and the use of the ubiquitous frog – a famous cure-all – which in this particular circumstance was to be boiled alive, in olive oil of course, and applied to the 'payn'd place'.

One olde English cure confirms a lot of my prejudices about the Soothmoothers. In the 1600s, when our English cousins got a throbbing toothache, they would apply the perspiration from a cat's anus to the tender spot, but only if the cat had been chased across a ploughed field immediately beforehand. I reckon that the efforts involved in securing the aforementioned sweat would make you forget all about your toothache. They're no' half clever those damn Englishers!

One in the Eye

Here, if your dare, is a seventeenth-century remedy by some anonymous Scottish quack for dimness of the eyes. Take 'salt armoniak, burnd and well brayd and mix it with ye pish of a young child and therewith anoint your eyes often'. Aye, well, you first!

Out, Damned Bonnet!

When Norman McLeod, a charismatic preacher from Stoer in Sutherland, led a band of his followers to St Ann's in Cape Breton Island in the early 1800s, he ran the strictest social regime imaginable. He was preacher, magistrate and teacher for the little community. His word was literally law. The patriarch once formally anathematised, or cursed, his wife's best bonnet because it was on the gaudy and garish side. McLeod and his team eventually moved on to settle in the Waipu district of New Zealand's North Island where thousands of the descendants of the colonists are found to this day.

Cairt Before the Cuddy

A sixteenth-century Act of Parliament urged the poor to seek sanctuary in the alms-houses of Scotland. Unfortunately, in the 1570s when the Act was published, none existed north of the Border.

Indigestion Guaranteed

Addressing a genealogy conference in Invercargill, New Zealand, a few years back, a full-blooded Maori dressed in grass skirt and face paints astonished his audience by claiming direct Scottish descent. He told the delegates that his grandfather had eaten a Scots missionary. Much earlier, when Buffalo Bill's Wild West Show hit Glasgow (August, 1904), one rumour about this colourful bunch which fascinated Glaswegians was that the culinary delicacy most enjoyed by the '100 North American Indians' in the party was stewed dog. In fact, the first meal in the city for the fierce warriors was rather tame fare – boiled chicken and milk pudding. Apparently the city's scabby hounds were not taking any chances, however, and were seen heading for the hills in packs.

A Great Might-Have-Been

Rolls-Weir – the name has a strange, unsatisfactory ring about it, does it not? Yet, in the early 1900s, that was very nearly the name of arguably the world's most famous car makers and the last word in motoring splendour. A possible deal between C S Rolls and the Weir Engineering Group of Glasgow collapsed at the last minute when Rolls chose Henry Royce as his partner. Perhaps the alliteration won the day.

Signing up for the Long Haul

In the days before steam trains or reliable sea transport, travelling to London was always considered such a serious matter that folk, particularly in the north of Scotland, would often make their wills before leaving. Even in the 1830s the journey by mail coach from London to Glasgow still took an average of 44 hours, and 180 horses, four in hand, were used in the course of the long haul north. It was illuminating in the hustle-bustle of the cool 1970s to get another wee reminder of a Scotland that was fast disappearing. A South Uist crofter was granted an increase in his fodder allowance from the Western Isles Education Committee. He sent his children to school by pony because there were no roads to his croft. During the so-called Crofters' War in the 1880s there was a sensation as a result of rating valuation when, on one occasion, a 2-month-old child was valued at sixpence while a collie puppy was assessed at a shilling.

There Goes the London Coach

The area now considered as Greater Glasgow was studded with collieries in the eighteenth and nineteenth centuries, operating at a variety of depths and always under testing conditions for the miners. In Shettleston, according to local historian Aileen Smart, the pit called Muirdibs was so shallowly dug that the colliers could hear the mail coach thundering along the road overhead.

A Road too Rough

Prehistoric man may have discovered the wheel but it was the 1500s before it was put to any sort of purposeful use for transport in Scotland. The first coach is reported to have been brought to Scotland from France by Mary Queen of Scots or, perhaps a few years earlier, by her mother, Mary of Guise. Before that, carts, which ventured on to the notoriously rough and desperately rutted roads of Scotland, were simply sleds.

By Hook or by Crook

It was Billy Connolly who, on his world tours, was in the habit of describing Bonnie Prince Charlie as that 'gay Italian dwarf'. More amusingly, and perhaps more accurately, he also suggested that the prince was the only figure in Scottish history to be named after three sheep dogs.

Ton-Mac' in the Mix

Sir Compton Mackenzie, a founder of the Scottish National Party and author of *Whisky Galore*, might also have been the world's first disc jockey. But, when the BBC offered him a record programme in 1927, he was off on his travels and his brother-in-law stood in. Mackenzie, who was actually born in Hartlepool, was another 'smart kid', learning Latin at the age of four and Greek by the age of nine.

There Was a Young Man from Seville . . .

It is thought that several hundred Spanish sailors from the ill-fated Armada were stranded around Scottish shores in 1588. As a result, security measures were introduced and, in Perth for example, Spaniards were classed alongside vagabonds and beggars as people who should be excluded by the town gatekeepers. The swarthy good looks of some folk in the Northern Isles is put down to an infusion of Iberian blood dating from the time of the stranded Spaniards.

The Wrecker's Prayer

The low-lying island of Sanday in Orkney has been the scene of numerous shipwrecks over the centuries. Tradition has it that locals were not averse, of a dark night, to drawing hapless vessels on to the rocks. In stormy weather even the minister is said to have prayed along these lines: 'If it is thy will that a ship should be wrecked this night, Lord send the vessel to the poor island of Sanday.'

Alex's Escapades

Perthshire minister Alexander Duff, the first foreign missionary of the Church of Scotland, was twice shipwrecked on his way to India. Having finally arrived safely, the Rev. Duff established schools for Hindus and Moslems and co-founded the *Calcutta Review.*

The Great Escape

Scots were among the most notorious slave owners in the 1700s, both in the sugar industry in the Caribbean and the tobacco trade in the American colonies. In the West Indies, one Scot even had the nasty habit of taking rebellious slaves out in a boat and dropping them, in leg-irons and chains, into the ocean. In Scotland in the Middle Ages, serfs and their families were bought and sold like cattle; in one instance, the Prior of Coldingham in Berwickshire is on record as having purchased the entire Hog family – father, sons and daughters – for £1. He probably didn't even believe he was getting a bargain. Latin documents of the time refer to *servi*, literally 'slaves', which leaves little doubt that such a class existed.

By the 1700s one practice was to transform a death sentence into lifetime slavery. Fishermen at Alloa dragged a brass collar from the muddy bottom of the Forth inscribed 'Alexander Stewart found guilty of death for theft, at Perth, 5 December 1701, but gifted as perpetual servant to Sir John Erskine of Alva.'

A Question of Priorities

Maybe our track record in the slave trade was being recalled the day the Maharajah of Hyderabad visited the famous Atlas railway works at Springburn, Glasgow, at the height of the railway boom. He was amazed to see thousands of workers streaming out of the yard at the lunchtime whistle and is said to have leapt to his feet, shouting at company officials, 'Your slaves are escaping!' Thanks to singer and renowned walker Jimmie Macgregor, one of Springburn's folk heroes, for that piece of lore.

The Atlas figures in another interesting tale of visiting celebrities. It's said that, on a tour to the works in 1942, George VI and Queen Elizabeth found that there was a new money-conscious generation in the making. When, surrounded by the products of heavy engineering, the Queen asked an apprentice what exactly he was making, the immediate reply came, 'Time an' a hauf, ma'am!'

Trailing the Fifers

Clydeside's pre-eminence as a leading world shipbuilding centre and home of Scotland's merchant fleet was a long time coming. In 1658 shipping records show that Glasgow boasted 12 vessels of up to 150 tons, while Fife could muster 39 similar vessels between the various burghs in the Kingdom. When the steamship revolution began, however, Glasgow soon made its impact. In January 1812 when Henry Bell launched his three-horsepower steamship *Comet* on the Clyde, it was the only such vessel in Europe. Within 20 years there were 70 steamers on the Clyde alone. Clydeside once had 60 shipyards from Glasgow to the Tail of the Bank and it has been estimated that, at its peak, the hammer's ding-dong produced a sixth of the world's tonnage. As with so much of Scotland's heavy industry, subsequent shrinkage was spectacular. By the mid 1990s there were only three yards left.

Hacking in the High Street

The illustrious Edinburgh University professor and philosopher Dugald Stewart (1753–1828) was so highly thought of by his students that one went as far as to suggest that there was 'eloquence in his very spitting'.

Hack of Disrespect

As far as the foul art of spitting goes, Edinburgh does, of course, have its own city-centre training ground. The Heart of Midlothian is a section of paving stone, laid in the shape of a heart, outside St Giles Cathedral in the High Street. It was the popular name for the old Tolbooth which stood on the spot, and citizens – much to the bemusement of tourists – can still be seen spitting on the slabs as a mark of contempt for authority. Or perhaps they are just bitter Hibees!

Putting Them on a Pedestal

Contrary to popular belief, the statue on top of the Jacobite monument at Glenfinnan, where the '45 uprising began, is not that of Bonnie Prince Charlie but that of a Jacobite officer whom the sculptor thought better represented the image of the Prince in the heather.

Difference of Opinion

It's strange how out of touch people can be with basic realities. A group of well-meaning folk suggested in the 1990s that the impressive statue of the Duke of Sutherland (a villain of the Clearances), which dominates the village of Golspie from nearby Ben Bhragie, should be floodlit. Locals with longer memories argued that a better course of action might be to break it into little pieces and use it for road bottoming.

The Makar Maks Do

Poet and founding figure of the twentieth-century Scottish literary 'renaissance', Hugh MacDiarmid (Christopher Grieve), seems always to have answered the muse – no matter the setting. On one legendary occasion, while drinking in a pub, he is reported to have demanded paper so he could jot down some lines which were forming. Lavvy paper was all that was available and the poet happily scribbled away. From such scenes Scotia's grandeur and gallus personality surely springs. Interestingly, the poem was titled 'Milkwort and Bog Cotton'.

The Cold Shoulder

In the early 1700s, Orkney islanders are said to have rescued an Inuit who was found exhausted and starving, his kayak having drifted thousands of miles across the North Atlantic from Greenland. This event is not as unlikely or rare as it might seem. Aberdeen University's Marischal Museum has in its collection an Inuit kayak, evidence of a similar visit to the north-east coast.

A Fine Pair of Knockers

One of the most impressive House of Commons characters is Black Rod, who raps on the door of the debating Chamber of the House of Commons and demands entry on behalf of the monarch. Before the Union of Parliaments of Scotland and England in 1707, Scotland had an 'Usher of the White Rod' who performed similar functions in Edinburgh. His role was lost – along with so many other aspects of the Scottish heritage – in the so-called merger, which was more of a takeover.

Lyte Relief in the Face of Catastrophe

Perhaps the most popular hymn ever written, and played most famously on the sloping deck of the *Titanic* as she slipped beneath the Atlantic, is 'Abide With Me', penned by Henry F. Lyte, a native of Ednam near Kelso. It's often forgotten, however, that the Titanic's band was not uniformly solemn in its final performance – they are also known to have included brighter melodies such as 'Alexander's Ragtime Band' in their parting repertoire.

For the thousands of emigrants from the Western Highlands and Islands during the 1800s, the saddest pipe tune of all was probably 'Cha till mituillead' (I Shall Return), which was played on the jetties as the emigrant ships set sail. It was truly an anthem for a displaced people, and heart-rending departure scenes were regularly reported in the Scottish press.

A Vision of the Future

Glasgow journalist Jack House, affectionately known as 'Mr Glasgow', had a memorable scoop in 1926 when he attended a press demonstration at Glasgow University of John Logie Baird's first workable television system. It has been suggested that other journalists were either bored or baffled, but Jack was the man who had the vision to see the significance of the breakthrough.

Blame the Kurds

'Teuchter' is generally accepted as a disparaging Lowland term for a Highlander, but the origin of the word is obscure. Some suggest it might derive from the word 'tutor', as it was used to describe the books of music for the great Highland bagpipe, but it has also been pointed out that the word is found in Kurdish.

CHAPTER 2
Coos, Comets and Scabby Dugs
The Wonderful World of Nature

'Gumsy' Robertson Shows the Way

The Scots of the Yukon – trappers, prospectors, hunters – were a notoriously hardy crew and canny to boot. A dentally challenged trapper with the splendid name of Nimrod Robertson, out in the wilds and hungry as a horse, shot a bear. How, in his toothless state, was Nimrod to deal with the bear's sinewy flesh? Undaunted, he is said to have hacked into the creature's mouth and dug out the appropriate gnashers needed to make a primitive set of falsers. He then ate the bear using its own teeth!

Spit out the Studs!

That is the sort of yarn which, I think, may have grown wings over a few glasses in the Malamut saloon. Equally impressive is the tale about Robert Campbell of Glen Lyon. Born in 1808, this tough Canadian frontiersman boiled up his snow shoes to make an edible paste and save his men from starvation. In an equally impressive piece of enterprise he avoided death by torture at the hands of a band of renegade Indians by reading to them at length from the Book of Joshua. The warriors are said to have been stunned into passivity by Bob's delivery, allowing him to make his escape.

Where Sheep Have Safely Over-Grazed

Before the arrival of sheep, scholars say that the glens and straths of the Scottish Highlands were carpeted in a spectacular profusion of flowers – in sharp contrast to the grey/green and bracken hue of today.

The Curse of Drink

A boozy Perthshire innkeeper may have been to blame for the Highland Clearances. Tradition has it that he bought some black-faced Linton sheep from the Borders but, being a neglectful drunk, he left them outside in the worst of weather; their survival astonished others and encouraged them to adopt the breed – and the rest is Highland history.

Scotland on the Move

Devastating mud slides are a feature of the twenty-first century that we usually associate with Central or South America and China. However, in 1629, a national appeal was launched after 16 small farms on fertile land between Falkirk and Stirling were destroyed when a huge area of moss slipped, turning the district into a 6-foot-deep quagmire. A similar event was reported in 1771 when 300 acres of Solway Moss, a thick, black mass, slid on to adjacent farm land, demolishing houses and drowning cattle. At Mormond Hill near Fraserburgh, an event took place in July 1789 which became known as the Mormond Hill Waterspout. Farmers, who had gone to the shore for sea sand, returned to find bridges swept away and burns converted into raging torrents. Great slabs of moss had been carried down the hill by the eruption of water from the hillside. The site proved a great novelty for visitors who came on to the hill to gaze into the vast chasms that appeared on the hillside – some of which were 20-feet deep.

Rock Solid Exports

Marble, quarried from around the fishing village of Portsoy in Banffshire and still on sale in local souvenir shops, was once exported to France to help in the construction of the Palace of Versailles.

Did the Earth Move?

Glasgow was one of several places shaken by a powerful earth tremor in 1984. Students of coincidence noted that Radio Two was playing the Beach Boys' 'Good Vibrations' at the time. It was not quite such a jovial matter in 1608 when an earthquake rocked Aberdeen and the kirk session declared that this was a clear warning from God about Sunday salmon fishing in the Dee.

When the earth moved for Scotland there were certainly some odd effects. In the summer of 1843 a strange phenomenon was reported at Leith where there was a sudden and mysterious in-rush of water at low tide, which retreated with equal swiftness. It seems likely that this mini tidal wave was the result of offshore seismic activity.

Well Met, Bearded Stranger

The story of our patriot king, Robert the Bruce, and his encounter with the persistent spider is well known but Bruce and the *Goat?* A local tradition suggests that, while still a fugitive in Kintyre, he slept in a cave on a wild winter's night and was 'warmed and comforted' by a goat that conveniently provided milk on tap. Thereafter, Bruce is said to have initiated a law forbidding anyone to impound a goat. A case of bleat, bleat and bleat again?

Pity the Poor Cuddies

The world-famous Mound in the heart of Edinburgh linking the Old and New Towns is an artificial hill that was begun in 1783 and which contains 1,501,000 cartloads of earth. How many horses were used in this mammoth operation is not recorded.

Artificial hills aside, Edinburgh has plenty of the genuine variety. In fact, our capital, which we Scots like to call the Athens of the North (not, as one cynic suggested, because of a shared problem with exhaust pollution) is, in fact, more like Rome, being built on seven hills – the highest being Arthur's Seat in Holyrood Park at 822 feet. There is some doubt as to the origin of the name, but one possible derivation is from the Gaelic – *Ard-n-Said* or 'Height of the Arrows'.

Solid Foundation

The vast granite quarry at Kemnay, Aberdeenshire, which supplied the stone for the new Scottish Parliament, also provided the raw material for the Thames Embankment in London.

The Battling Codfathers

The occasional disappearance of fish from waters around Scotland – long before the man with the scarily appropriate name, Herr Fischler, the EU Fisheries Commissioner, put in his oar – was often attributed to the spilling of fishermen's blood in the sea during the all too frequent disputes over catches.

Fish on a Plate

After dock trials of the engines Cunard liner *Queen Mary* at Clydebank in 1936, five stones of fish, including herring, saith, cod and flounder, were found to have been sucked through filtration grills.

Salmon Tales

Today, when the wild Atlantic salmon appears to be teetering on the edge of extinction, it's difficult to believe that salmon was so plentiful in Scotland a few hundred years ago that, apart from being an important export item, it had become an almost monotonous meal. Apprentices demanded in their rules that, under no circumstances, were they to be served salmon on more than 3 days a week! Critics of Prince Charles were stunned to discover in 2002 that, in the 1960s while he was attending Gordonstoun school, the heir to the throne had been writing to the government warning of the depletion of wild salmon stocks.

From Out of the Ice Pack

In the Hebrides, jellyfish are known by the Gaelic word for congealed sea (*muir-teuchd*), an idea possibly relating to vague rumours and travellers' tales of the existence of polar ice.

It's the Little People!

The Lewis chessmen, 4 inches tall and made from walrus tusk, are considered the finest medieval chess pieces so far discovered anywhere in Europe. They were uncovered by a crofter in a cattle scrape at Uig Bay in 1831 and terrified him because he believed them to be nothing less than the fairy folk of Celtic legend. The images of the chessmen were immortalised in the children's cartoon, *Noggin The Nog*.

Attack of the Killer Midgies

Midgies have been a blight on Scottish tourism since long before the first Thomas Cook tour came north of the Border in 1846. In his struggle for Scottish independence, Robert Bruce is said to have been troubled almost as much by midgie-attacks as by the English and Queen Victoria permitted her house guests to smoke in the salons at Balmoral simply to keep the midgies at bay. By 1944, the problem had become so acute that Scots Secretary of State, Tom Johnston, suggested adopting anti-midge techniques developed by the US military – just one of a thousand supposed remedies which have failed miserably. It's said that, in the Western Highlands, ancestral home of the midgie, clan chieftains – generally a pretty uncouth bunch – had one particularly gruesome form of torture. Victims were bound to a stake by the lochside and left to the attentions of the clouds of midgies. Madness, it's said, was the normal outcome, with death not unheard of.

There are 37 species of the dreaded midgie and it is the females who perform the bloodsucking. Surprisingly perhaps, humans get a low rating in the blood stakes – deer, cattle, rabbits and dogs being much more docile and less likely to flail their arms about like the demented tourists.

Thereby Hangs a Tail

At the end of the nineteenth century, an ox of quite enormous dimensions was sold by Colonel Hamilton of Pencaitland, East Lothian, to a Shropshire army butcher. The animal was reportedly 16 feet long, 10 feet in girth and stood over 5 foot 8 inches tall. The genuine article or just a load of old bull?

What Did Willie Know?

In *The Comedy of Errors* (Act III, sc. 2), William Shakespeare confirmed the generally held European view in the Early Modern Period that Scotland was a barren, forlorn location. He compared the landscape in its nakedness to the palm of the hand but had he ever properly examined the palm of a Highlander? Hairy knees were only half the story.

Flocking Together

In an early example of wildlife conservation, the slaughter of heron, which had been 'frequent and common' in Fife, Kinross and the Carse of Gowrie, was banned in 1600 for three years as it was said that 'only a few or nane' birds were left.

The first animal to be bought by Edinburgh Zoo was a gannet, which cost 18p and now appears on the crest of the Royal Zoological Society of Edinburgh. The solan goose or gannet, found in enormous numbers on the Bass Rock in the estuary of the River Forth, was once sold in quantity to the citizens of Edinburgh where it graced many a dinner table.

Your Bears Are Scary

The great Caledonian bear – a Scottish animal like the wolf and the wild boar, long extinct – was shipped to Rome in sturdy iron cages during the centuries of Roman occupation to provide 'sport' for the citizens in the great gladiatorial arenas.

Who Moved That Island?

Scotland officially has 787 islands ranging from wee principalities in their own right, such as Skye, Arran and Orkney Mainland, to sea-washed skerries 'capable of supporting a sheep'. Loch Lomond contains some 30, ranging from outcrops to the two-mile-square Inchmurrin. However, over the centuries, there has been a persistent legend concerning a mysterious, mobile thirty-first island which appears and disappears in the morning mist and evening twilight.

Leven's Eleven

Here's a piece of numerical trivia which is bound to impress. Loch Leven in Kinross-shire, where Mary Queen of Scots was imprisoned in the island castle, is magically bound up with the number eleven. The loch has eleven islands, it is eleven miles in the round and is reputed to have eleven rivers or streams flowing into it.

The King's Beasties

Stranded whales were so common in the Forth estuary in early medieval Scotland that David I gave the rights to all these valuable creatures to the Augustinian monks of Holyrood.

Bonnie and Blooming

If you're looking for the most spectacular heather hill in Scotland then steer away from the predictable parts of the Western Highlands and head for Drumtochty Hill, north of Laurencekirk in Kincardineshire. And how do we know this? In his classic portrait of Mearns farm life, *Sunset Song*, Lewis Grassic Gibbon has his young lovers visit the hill where Ewan tells Chris that 'in summer it came deeper with the purple of heather' than any other brae in Scotland.

Versatile Bloom

At the Neolithic community of Skara Brae in Orkney, archaeologists found rope made from heather. Ale, bedding, tea, thatch and firewood were among the many other uses of our ubiquitous national bloom.

With all the tragic/romantic outpourings which followed the Jacobite defeat at Culloden, it's an interesting observation that, since the defeat of Bonnie Prince Charlie's army at Drumossie Moor, heather has failed to flourish on the scene of the conflict. Cynics will tell you that it's simply down to a change of land use but the White Heather Club will tell that it will never grow until the young pretender gains his lawful place. Could be a long wait, unless they are thinking of John Swinney!

The Paps Are in Sight

An old Glasgow tradition suggests that the distant Paps of Jura are visible from the city's West End on Glasgow Fair Saturday. Incidentally, those imaginative folk, who believe in world conspiracies, ghosts, ghoulies and a Scottish World Cup victory one day, are convinced that a tunnel links the island of Jura off the west coast of Scotland with the Jura region of France. If that's the case, then why did they bother to build the Channel Tunnel?

The Long and the Short o' it

The ribbon or bootlace worm is the longest of all living creatures. One specimen measuring around 180 feet was found off the east coast of Scotland: Gulliver's bootlace and no mistake.

Tropical Clydebank

In terms of unusual fish colonies, you need look no further than my home patch in Clydebank. In the 1960s abandoned goldfish – prizes from the local funfair – flourished in the waters of the Forth and Clyde Canal – the legendary 'Nolly' – in a stretch of water near Kilbowie Road, artificially warmed by the hot water outflow from the turbines of the Singer sewing machine plant. Another unusual canal occupant was discovered at Kirkliston near Edinburgh during the construction of the Union Canal in the early 1800s – it was the tusk of a mammoth, nearly 5 feet long, discovered under 25 feet of rock and soil.

Lapping up the Challenge

In 1789, citizens of Aberdeen were asked to pay 25 guineas towards the annual board and lodgings for the council chambers cat, which had been brought in because of rat infestation.

Game On – Thanks to the Icefields

Glacial sands from the meltwater streams which flowed under the Great Caledonian ice sheet 18,000 years ago help give the Borders some of the best-drained rugby pitches in the world.

The Beasts of Cumbernauld

Medieval Scots historian Hector Boece wrote in the early 1500s of the wild cattle of Scotland – white, fierce, untameable creatures with lion-like manes. They are thought to have been among the original inhabitants of the Great Caledonian Forest, now sadly a few birches in some lost glen. Some 30 years after Boece's death came the last mention of these almost mythical beasts when it was suggested that most of the remaining 'white kye and bulls' had been slain in Lord Fleming's forest of Cumbernauld.

The Biggest Drip of All

Broxburn, West Lothian, was the unlikely setting, during the reign of Queen Victoria, for a short-lived Eighth Wonder of the World when a sturdy 100-foot-long icicle formed from a viaduct on the Union Canal and quickly became a tourist attraction. A picture postcard was even produced to mark the phenomenon.

An Early Start in the Garden

King David I, who reigned from 1124 to 1153, was probably the first Scottish monarch to take a serious interest in gardening. According to the chroniclers, he often used his leisure time for the cultivation of his garden and the 'philosophical amusement' of budding and engrafting trees.

It Surely Is a Dog's Life

The Covenanting army, passing through Aberdeen in 1639, executed scores of dogs. On a previous visit to the town by the Covenanters, resident cavalier ladies had mocked the blue ribbon awarded to each soldier by decorating their pets with similar ribbons. The pooches paid a terrible price.

It seems dogs continued to suffer in the Granite City. Peter Gibb called his two dogs Calvin and Luther in 1786 as a ridicule of the Protestant townsfolk. But the joke backfired and the dogs were publicly executed by the Proddy mob. Another difficult time for the Scottish dog population in the 1700s came as the result of an Edinburgh butcher's dog going mad. Magistrates ordered the slaughter of all such animals that wandered the streets. Pets, and even dogs which led the blind, were to be locked up or suffer the same fate. A shilling bounty was placed on the head of each mutt, which encouraged dog-hunting gangs to roam the streets of the capital.

And Here I Thought it Was the 'Es'!

Huge bouquets of flowers giving off carbonic acid were blamed for headaches and other pains suffered by dancers after grand society balls in different parts of Scotland during the 1840s.

Bringing Home the Bacon

In his later years, Lord Gardenstone, one of the nation's top nineteenth-century legal brains, kept pigs and trained one to follow him about like a dog. As a piglet, it shared his bed and, as it grew, he permitted the pig to stay in his room. His clothes provided a couch for the pig and his lordship was kept comfortably warm by the slumbering porker. What the chronicles remain ominously silent about is whether the animal was house-trained.

Darkness at Noon

One of the earliest reports of a total eclipse of the sun comes in the *Orkneyinga Saga*. It recalls the darkness at noon in 1263 as the Norse fleet prepared to sail from the green isles to do battle – unsuccessfully as it transpired – with the Scots at Largs.

Waiter, What's This Snail Doing in my Ginger

According to some sources the legendary west of Scotland plea of 'Gie's a slug' (of any refreshing liquid) has its origins in a historic consumers' rights case in Paisley in the 1930s when a partially decomposed snail was found in a bottle of ginger beer in a local café. It set the pattern for consumer legislation the world over.

Stobcross Street Grunts

Political correctness and concern for animal welfare were not high on the list of priorities for Glasgow tea tycoon Thomas Lipton. Every day, two pigs were driven up from the dock to his Glasgow shop in Stobcross Street, wearing a banner which declared, 'I'm on my way to Liptons – The Best Place in Town for Bacon'.

Fuelling Their Passion

Aberdeenshire farmer and talented diarist Charlie Allan recounted the story of a four-year-old boy watching his farmer dad rubbing petrol on the hin' end of their sheepdog, Bess, to keep male dogs at bay when she was in heat. The wee chap accepted this procedure, in the matter-of-fact way that 4-year-olds do, but appeared at the kitchen door minutes later with a worried look and declared, 'Dad, come quick! Bess has run oot o' petrol and anither dog is gieing her a push across the yard.'

Critics, Critics Everywhere

The great twentieth-century Scottish poet Norman McCaig carried an albatross as well as an oyster-catcher around his neck for 30 years. In a published poem, he described the colourful oyster-catcher, a bird of the water margin, as having yellow legs when they are, in fact, the brightest orange. For three decades, he had to live with this error until it was corrected in his *Collected Poems*.

At Least the Dog Was Chuffed

After Lord Aberdeen adopted the rather daunting and clumsy title of Aberdeen and Temair in 1915, his wife sent out a card with a picture of herself and her pet dog signed – 'Ishbel Aberdeen and Temair'. A friend wrote back thanking her for the lovely portrait of Lady Aberdeen and her dog Temair.

High Tide and No Mistake

There is strong evidence that a tsunami, or tidal wave, caused by a major land movement along the coast of Norway, swept the eastern shores of Scotland in Neolithic times. Middens left by the hunter-gatherer people appear to have been overwhelmed by a catastrophic tidal wave, the debris from which has been discovered at locations as far apart as Inverness and Fife. The discovery of a vast meteor crater on the bed of the North Sea in recent years indicates another means by which great inundations might have occurred.

Cheeky Yarn

Ecclefechan-born historian Thomas Carlyle once told Queen Victoria that the coast road from Creetown to Gatehouse of Fleet was the most beautiful in her realm. Vicky asked if there was no other as impressive.

'Yes, ma'am,' said the brass-necked wordsmith, 'the road from Gatehouse of Fleet to Creetown.' Was the monarch amused, we wonder? It was the sort of cheek which, in centuries past, would have got you thrown into the Bloody Tower.

A Monstrous Allegation

In March 1941, Italian newspapers claimed that bombing raids in Scotland had been so intense that the Loch Ness monster had been struck by a direct hit.

No Mercy for Ratty

The guid folk of Caithness developed a rather horrendous and definitely non-PC way of disposing of rats. They fried small pieces of cork in grease which the rats then gobbled up lustily. When they drank water the cork swelled and burst the rodents' intestines. Nice ... It was an interesting tradition of neighbouring Sutherland that the county was devoid of rats 'because of something mystical in the air'.

Room for One More Chuckie?

The mineralogist Robert Jamieson (1774–1854), as Keeper of Edinburgh University Museum, broke all sorts of records as he gathered – admittedly with some official help but also at great personal cost – a vast collection of 40,000 rocks and minerals, 10,000 fossils, 8,000 birds and many thousands of insects

Out of Sight

The fossil of a 3-foot long, salamander-like creature which lay in a drawer for 30 years at the University of Glasgow was identified in 2002 as a 'missing link' in the evolution of fish into vertebrates, including humans. *Pederpes inneyae* was found near Dumbarton in 1971 but surely the three-decade wait for recognition was only a short-term irritation – the creature trudged around the land and water shallows some 350 million years ago.

Nothing Like a Guid Greet

The last will and testament of Mary Queen of Scots was held for many years by the Scots College in Paris. Some of the words on this historic document had been smudged, others blotted out by the sad queen's tears or so said the romantics. By all accounts, Mary did indeed enjoy a good greet. In her emotional encounters with John Knox, she occasionally ran out of handkerchiefs as the old greybeard ranted and raved. Mary is also said to have burst into tears when she saw the scrawny old nags provided for her party of relatives and courtiers on her arrival in Scotland in 1561 to take the reins of government. Observers commented on the startling contrast with the finely bred horses which she was accustomed to at the French court.

It would seem that circumstances had improved a little by the time of her wedding to Henry Lord Darnley four years later. It is recorded that, during the marriage procession, a gent called Cumin of Culter in Aberdeenshire, anxious to show off his personal wealth, had his horse shod with silver shoes. They were so lightly nailed, however, that, when the horse was asked to prance – as they often were on ceremonial occasions – the shoes fell off, resulting in a mad scramble by the Edinburgh mob looking for part of this unexpected windfall. Nowadays, of course, when Aberdonians want to show off their personal wealth they either buy a four-trak, all-weather vehicle or take out an annual subscription to a flash fitness club.

Hey, Black Beauty, a Word in Yer Lug

The clandestine Society of the Horseman's Word, which seems to have originated in Scotland and conferred on its brotherhood the mystical powers needed to control horses, had bizarre notions about how this 'power' might be obtained. On the Orkney island of North Ronaldsay, they believed that a nail taken from a coffin in which a body had lain for seven years would, if pushed into the imprint made by a horseshoe in the earth, paralyse the horse that made the mark and ready the animal to obey your every command. Personally, I've always found an extra strong mint works wonders.

No Proud Boast

Six young Confederate cavalry officers – all of Scottish descent – met in Tennessee around Christmas 1865 to form a club which took its trappings from the so-called Horse Whisperers. The organisation was to become the notorious Ku-Klux Klan.

Steady on Your Lordship

The horse was always an animal of prime importance in Scotland, as we see in an eighteenth-century letter from Ayrshire's 10th Earl of Eglinmont on the eve of a duel to the death. He told his younger brother in a classic piece of advice, 'Don't neglect horse-shoeing if you love Scotland.' He was perhaps getting a little overwrought at the prospect of the coming confrontation.

Hand it to the Astronomers

Astronomical description and measurement was in its infancy in the 1600s, as is evidenced by a report in 1664. A comet crossed Scotland from south-east to north-west on 6 December. It was generally agreed to be terrible in appearance and 'about the breadth of a reasonable man's hand'. Show me a reasonable man and we'll get a measure.

Singing Sands

It was a famous Cromarty geologist, Hugh Miller, who first reported that the white, dry sand on the beaches of the Isle of Eigg produces a musical tone when walked upon. We still have a long way to go, however, to match the sand of Oregon in the United States which is said to squeak, according to one writer, with the 'highpitched bark of distant Chihuahuas'.

Overwhelmed!

One of the most unusual pleas for government financial help in the seventeenth century came from Alexander Kinnaird, of Culbin on the Moray Firth, whose country house, yards and orchards were over-whelmed by blown sand. Amazingly, for years afterwards, the tops of the fruit trees, peeking above the sand dunes, continued to bud and blossom.

Further down the east coast at Forvie in Aberdeenshire, at the mouth of the River Ythan, is the fifth largest sand system in the United Kingdom and, beneath the dunes – now a paradise for wild birds and plants – is a buried medieval village, the only remnants of which are the ruined walls of the parish church.

Wood for the Trees

Scientists have discovered that some pine trees still thriving in the glens of the Western Highlands took root before Columbus sailed across the Atlantic in 1492.

By the 1400s, however, we know that wood was already scarce in Scotland. In 1457 James II ordered every freeholder to create a park for deer and to plant at least one acre with trees. Yet, by the time Dr Johnson and his mate James Boswell made their famous journey to the Western Isles in 1755, they found the countryside 'naked of trees'.

Moving the Pulpit

The tree under which John Knox was reputed to have held the first Reformed Communion in Renfrewshire (1556) – at Finlaystone, near Port Glasgow – was blocking natural light to a house. So, in 1900, it was uprooted and dragged some 40 yards along a track of railway sleepers to a more open location. It is poignant that the sermon preached by the old greybeard on the day was said to have been one of his most moving.

Anyone for Meerkats?

When the famous zoo, Wombwell's Menagerie, was broken up at auction in Scotland in 1872, there was tremendous interest in the 90 lots, which included lions, tigers, elephants and emus. The Earl of Rosebery snapped up a bargain with a successful bid of £1 for a racoon.

Blame Mercator

It's a surprising fact that Newcastle is further north than Scotland's most southerly point, the tip of the Mull of Galloway.

The Hills Are Alive

One of Scotland's most popular tourist areas is the Trossachs. The name is Gaelic and means 'the bristling country'. Whether bristling with mountain peaks or impenetrable undergrowth we can but speculate although it is certain that, these days, particularly during summer weekends, it positively bristles with humanity.

Stop – and Drop

Some of the greenest hollows in the Scottish mountains are the well-manured legacy of the days of cattle droving. Many such overnight 'stances' on the route to the trysts or cattle sales can be identified.

The Cleansing of the Clyde

The recovery of the Clyde in the twenty-first century from its days as a fetid artery of the Industrial Revolution is well illustrated not only by the reappearance of salmon and the occasional seal but also by the increase in the number of wild birds. John Molloy, gardener at the riverside Scottish Exhibition and Conference Centre, has reported 83 species in the vicinity, including that impressive angler, the osprey.

CHAPTER 3

Fechters – Bonnie or Otherwise

The Scrapping, Argumentative Scot

Sneaking up on the Lion

Weather is no respecter of rank or station. In 1173 William the Lion, King of Scots (1143–1214) was doing what most Scots monarchs have felt the need to do from time to time – invading England. Near Alnwick in Northumberland he was huckled by a group of Yorkshire knights who emerged unexpectedly from the summer mist. It was reported that William had mistaken them for his own forces. He was cairted off as prisoner to Henry II at Northampton with his feet tied beneath the belly of his horse. Altogether not one of Scotland's great days. William was subsequently obliged to sign the Treaty of Falaise in which he accepted Henry II of England as his overlord. The whole affair sounds distinctly unchivalrous.

Getting in Among Them

The penetration of the Jacobite army as far as Derby in 1745 is widely regarded as the most brazen and audacious invasion of England by a Scots military force. However, in 1216, Alexander II's army reached Dover.

The Cold War

The abortive Jacobite coup of 1708 had no grand plans to march on London and parade triumphantly down Whitehall. Its more modest strategic goal was to occupy the collieries of Newcastle and freeze London into submission.

Sabre Rattling in the Blue Toon

Up until the Second World War, prison officers at Peterhead – one of Britain's toughest penal establishments, saved from closure in 2002 by a national campaign – were armed with sabres to keep inmates in line.

A Bridge Not Far Enough for Davie

Warfare was a way of life for long periods of the Middle Ages and the best way to secure a living was to capture a member of the opposing gentry during battle and ransom him off to his family. It was the equivalent of a lottery win. English squire John Coupland hit the jackpot and set himself up for life at the Battle of Neville's Cross, in October 1346, by taking David II, King of Scots, into custody. The king, his army evaporating round about him, was taken prisoner while hiding under a bridge, near Durham, but managed to knock out two of Coupland's teeth in the struggle.

A Dram too Soon for Papay

In October 1918, the far-flung island of Papa Westray celebrated the end of the First World War prematurely when a statement circulated in Orkney indicating that Germany had surrendered. Most of Orkney considered the source unreliable but, on Papa Westray, farm workers were summoned from the fields, treated to a dram at the big hoose and given a half-day holiday. According to the local paper, 'the whole island gave way to merrymaking'. The actual signing of the Treaty of Versailles came in June 1919.

Melodies from the Front Line

Eighteenth-century Perthshire-born General John Reid tried to combat the stress of military campaigns by composing flute sonatas in his tent. He left his fortune to the University of Edinburgh to endow a chair of music.

The Lost Legion of Durham

One of Scotland's least known military tragedies was the death of 1,600 Covenanter prisoners captured during the Battle of Dunbar in 1650. They were held in Durham Cathedral, pending transportation to the American Colonies, but suffered terribly in an outbreak of dysentery. Only a few hundred were eventually sent overseas.

Straight to the Bottom

Scotland suffered a severe blow in 1481 when several pieces of state-of-the-art weaponry and field artillery, a gift from Sigismund, Archduke of Austria, were lost at sea. Naturally, James III was disappointed but he must have given serious thought to omens because, in 1460, an exploding cannon had killed his father at the siege of Roxburgh.

Pull the Trigger, Patrick

At the Battle of Brandywine (1777), during the American War of Independence, a Scots officer and marksman, Patrick Ferguson, holding the brand-new breech-loading rifle which he himself had developed, found a senior American officer in his sights. But he refused to do the dishonourable thing and fire – because the Yankee rebel had his back to him. Later Ferguson discovered that his target had been none other than George Washington.

Still on the theme of missed opportunities, after John Balliol was perceived to have sold out the Scottish nation in the thirteenth century, it was unthinkable that any future King of Scots could carry the cursed handle of John. In 1390, John, Earl of Carrick, eldest son of Robert II, was to be crowned and there was much debate about his new name. To my mind there was a great opening here for a King Andrew or King Colin but, rather unimaginatively, the policy-makers plumped for Robert III.

Ye Bowmen of Olde England

The secret weapon in the armies of medieval England was, perhaps surprisingly, not the chivalrous knights in armour or the massive siege engines but the longbow. England's archers won them battles as far afield as Agincourt (1415) and against the Scots at Neville's Cross (1346). Their accuracy is said to be reflected in the number of one-eyed Scots found in the military annals.

Last Orders, Gentlemen

When 500 Jacobites, under the Earl of Cromarty, swarmed into Dunrobin Castle near Golspie in 1746, it was the last recorded storming of a fortress on the UK mainland.

Small but Deadly

During the First World War two special battalions of the Highland Light Infantry were formed specially to cater for small Glaswegians – bonnie wee fechters all – averaging 5 feet in height. Called the Bantams, they were also known to the Germans as the fearless 'Demon Dwarves'.

Jock the Revolutionary

Hours after the violent explosion of the Russian Revolution in 1917, the Council of Soviets met to appoint three Honorary Presidents. The first two nominations were predictable: Vladimir Lenin and Leon Trotsky. The third was John Maclean, a Glasgow schoolteacher who had been spreading the word of revolution in Scotland. This recognition of Maclean's support was no passing fancy. In 1979 the Soviet Union produced a postage stamp bearing Maclean's image.

Scots at the Helm

The extent of the Caledonian influence in Tzarist Russia is well illustrated by the fact that *two* Scots could lay claim to the title of founding father of the Russian navy – Admiral Thomas Gordon and Samuel Greig, who both achieved significant naval successes for the Tsars in the 1700s. Around this time there were said to be 40 naval officers of senior rank with Scottish roots in Russian naval service.

Putting the Wind up the Warhorses

The medieval Scottish armoury included, perhaps surprisingly, rattles. These were pots, which were filled with small stones, fixed to the end of long poles and then shaken furiously. They were used – with some measure of success apparently – to disrupt English cavalry charges.

Death-Dealing our Specialty

Carronades, highly effective pieces of artillery used at both Waterloo and Trafalgar, were named in honour of their manufacturing plant, the Carron Iron Works at Falkirk. The design was developed by Scots Lieutenant-General Robert Melville, who also oversaw their manufacture. The first shrapnel shells were also developed at the Carron works and tested on the mud flats of the Forth.

Das Boot Drops Anchor

Many momentous and tragic events unfolded around Scotland, during the Second World War, but local folklore in Sutherland tells of a remarkable social event at the height of the conflict. The crew from a German U-boat are said to have landed on the shores of Loch Eriboll for a picnic on a fine summer's morning.

The Tartan Zimmer Brigade

When Bonnie Prince Charlie returned to Rome after the failure of the '45 uprising, he had a lot of correspondence to catch up with. Among the pile of letters was a dispatch from Frederick the Great of Russia saying that all of Europe had been astonished by Charlie's bold enterprise. He wrote, 'For tho' Alexander and other heroes have conquered with inferior armies, you are the only one who has ever engaged in such an attempt without any.' A bit harsh on the brave Highlanders who fell at Culloden, but we know what he means.

The Highland army during the '45, apart from its fighting men, had its share of pensioners and striplings in the ranks. The Marquis of Tullibardine was so ill with gout when he ceremonially raised Bonnie Prince Charlie's standard at Glenfinnan that he had to be supported by two companions. And the ancient Glenbuckett was reported to have been bent double in his saddle as the Prince's army passed through Macclesfield en route for Derby. Groups of boys, aged about 12, were also in this motley crew and their task was to go armed with knives into the thick of the cavalry action to cut and injure the legs of enemy horses. Dirty and very dangerous work.

Edinburgh Throws its Weight Around

Civic rivalry in Scotland is usually at its most intense between the venerable Edinburgh and the young upstart Glasgow. But it's an established fact that, over the centuries, there has been little love lost between Edinburgh and its seaport at Leith. In the 1400s, an order levied a 40-shilling fine and loss of trading rights for a year on any Edinburgh merchant taking a Leith resident into partnership.

Nothing New under the Sun

We tend to think of ethnic cleansing as a relatively new aspect of warfare and very un-British – but we delude ourselves. In the 1520s, Scottish towns and villages were devastated by raids organised by the Earl of Surrey, whose openly declared aim was to create a 12-mile-deep 'desert' or sterile zone inside the Scots Border. And, of course, we have the quote attributed to an early Caledonian patriot, Calgacus, when he took on and was defeated by the Romans at the Battle of Mons Graupius, which has chilling echoes right into the twenty-first century – 'They make a desert and call it peace.'

Wattie the Scapegoat

By all accounts, Sir Walter Scott and his romantic writings about misty glens and doughty freedom fighters had dramatic effects in the American South in the mid-nineteenth century. On one occasion, he was blamed by Mark Twain for the outbreak of the American Civil War.

The War Mentality

Many of the nuns, who helped establish the convent of St Catherine of Siena at the Meadows in Edinburgh in 1517, were the wives of men who had fallen at the Battle of Flodden two years previously. Flodden has always been portrayed, inevitably perhaps, as a total rout for Scotland with the king, James IV, and the majority of his nobles slain, not to mention thousands of his peasant army. Less often reported is the footnote by an English historian referring to the fact that the returning remnants of the shattered Scottish army took 60 English prisoners back across the Border with them.

In the immediate aftermath of the slaughter of the Scots at Flodden Field, an English invasion was expected hourly. Edinburgh merchants, who had been left in charge of the city, ordered that all females, on pain of banishment, should cease from crying and lamenting in the street. It was giving the citizens the heebie-jeebies or, as the chronicles put it, their weeping and wailing was 'causing a dispiriting effect' and hindering preparations for further war.

O'er She Goes!

One of the most spectacular actions of the war between America and Britain in the early 1800s came about when Sir Allan Napier McNab, a proud Scots descendant living in Canada, sent an American steamship tumbling over Niagara Falls in flames. This was in response to a raid on Canadian territory.

Throwing Some Light on the Matter

An Act of the Scottish Parliament, dated 1455, provides fascinating detail on the operation of beacon fires that were lit across southern Scotland to warn of English invasion. The typical beacon was probably a 'long and strong tree' set up with a sturdy iron crosspiece at its summit from which metal frames were hung to contain one or more tar barrel. One bale, or faggot, was to be lit to warn of the approach of an English force; two bales were to alert the capital that the English were 'coming indeed'; when four bales were seen blazing side by side, it was time to lock up your daughters and strap on your reinforced codpiece because this meant that the enemy (not surprisingly, a word synonymous with the 'English') were flocking over the Border.

During the Napoleonic Wars, the system of Border beacons still operated to warn of French invasion. On one occasion, the accidental ignition of a beacon prompted the lighting of all the others and, for a few hours, the whole nation was on a red alert with thousands of volunteers rushing to their battle stations.

Booty on a Plate

After the Battle of Dunbar (1296), Edward I, Hammer of the Scots, could only rustle up enough booty in the Scottish capital to fill three small treasure chests. In his inventory, the most interesting item was what was described as a 'Griffin's Egg' – broken but patched with silver – which the English king thought he might trundle out as a bit of a novelty on state occasions. Received wisdom is that it was probably a coconut or an ostrich egg.

The Raggle-Taggle Army

When Napoleon contemptuously described the Brits as a nation of shopkeepers rather than fighters, he had clearly forgotten the Scottish dimension. Not for the first time Nappy was talking through a hole in his fancy cocked hat. In July 1484, a peasant army, made up principally of market traders, defeated the rebellious Duke of Albany and the 'Black Douglas' at Lochmaben as that deadly duo tried to rally support for an insurrection.

Ending the Bounce Game

George Elliot, a career soldier and laird's son from Stobo in the Borders, didn't forget his agricultural background when he was appointed commander of the Rock of Gibraltar in 1779. Under siege by the Spanish (nice to know some things never change), Geordie ordered the streets to be ploughed up to lessen the ricochet effect of cannonballs during the bombardment.

With a Song in Your Hat

One of Robbie Burns's most enigmatic songs is a strange wee ditty entitled 'Cock Up Your Beaver', which, we're told, refers to sprucing up a beaver hat. However, any alternative interpretations will be welcomed.

Scots descendants fighting at the Alamo in the struggle for Texan independence, among them Crockett, Bowie and piper John McGregor, are said to have had their own marching song – 'Green Grow The Rashes O'. Of course, the boys were marching nowhere but to an early grave. However, surrounded by Santa Anna's army, they are recorded as having belted it out good-style and, as a result, the Mexicans, thinking this was a defiant chant from the defenders, coined the word *Gringo* to describe all Americans. Well, can you come up with a better explanation?

The Melodies of Warfare

A magical soundbite from Scotland's military past is included in the famous *Complaynt of Scotland*, a political treatise printed in 1548 at St Andrews and – here's a surprise – a document which was hostile to

England. The section of the treatise which interests us portrays the sound of guns during a sea battle. Thus: 'Cannons and gunnies mak mony hideous crak – duf, duf, duf, duf-duf; the falcons cryit – tirduf, tirduf, tirduf, tirduf; the small artailye cryit – tik-tak, tik-tak, tik-tak.' Onomatopoeia's the business, is it not?

The Musket's Mother

When cannon were first used against the Highland clans, it's said that the men from the glens – in superstitious dread – threw themselves to the ground as, what they called, 'the musket's mother' spoke.

Not so Merry Men

Street riots were commonplace in sixteenth-century Edinburgh but perhaps the most spectacular episode of the period happened when magistrates banned a traditional performance of the *Robin Hood* pageant and general mayhem ensued.

No' Stovies Again!

Prison riots are no modern phenomenon. In 1692 prisoners at the Tolbooth in the Canongate, Edinburgh, rioted and took possession of the prison, complaining about the quality of the food.

Viking Nancy Boys

The Norse have always had a bad press because of their Dark Ages raping and pillaging exploits. But they did bring some unexpected aspects of wider European culture to Scotland. They combed their hair regularly, washed more than was good for them, set aside Saturday as bath days and frequently de-loused themselves. Cynical Scottish monks thought all this cleanliness was simply a device by the horned and horny warriors to seduce gullible Scots lasses. (Scholars will tell you that it was the Anglo-Saxons who wore the horns, but that was too good an alliteration to bypass!)

Blitz on the Northeast

Surprisingly, perhaps, Aberdeen was Scotland's most regularly bombed community during the Second World War – the Luftwaffe launched 34 raids on the city. While none compared with the scale and catastrophe of the Clydebank Blitz, a number were, according to reports, 'determined and damaging'. Peterhead and Fraserburgh frequently experienced the unwelcome visitors, each having 23 attacks, and, along with Aberdeen, earned the description as Scotland's 'front-line towns'. Three George medals were won by Aberdeen citizens during the raids. Even far-flung Wick lost 15 people – including seven children – in a single aircraft raid in July 1940.

War 'Crimes'

The Roxy picture house in Hamilton was fined £25 in October 1943 for not showing its quota of British films. Another unusual Second World War offence involved two Renfrewshire boys who were each fined 10 shillings for throwing lighted matches at each other during the blackout, presumably drawing the might of German bomber command towards the west of Scotland's large population centres. Aye, well, rules are rules.

Scotland's first genuine blackout of the Second World War took place in August 1939. The seriousness of the situation only came home to many Scots when it transpired that, because of the crisis, several pubs were to close two hours early, at the unhealthily early hour of 8 p.m.

Terror of the Trenches

Lt Col. Sir Iain Colquhoun, a Flashman character and clan chief of the Colquhouns of Luss on Loch Lomondside, was an all-round good egg, boxing champion and fearless First World War fighter, who is reputed to have kept a fairly tame lion in the trenches with him as a pet.

Dead Giveaway

In 1591, when the Bonny Earl o' Moray, commemorated in song and legend, was besieged at Donibristle Castle in Fife, he was forced to flee in the darkness as the buildings of the castle were set alight. He might have made his escape but for the fact that the plumage on his helmet caught fire. He was murdered on the shore by his enemies who had followed his fiery progress through the night.

Sleepy Hollow

A modern exhibition, outlining the Borders Battle of Philiphaugh, in 1645 when the Marquis of Montrose defeated the Covenanters, is staged at Halliwell's Close Museum in Selkirk. It modestly describes the confrontation as the only day anything happened in Selkirk.

Fine Detail

John Barbour, a fourteenth-century Scots writer and academic, had the modern war correspondent's sharp eye for detail. In his work *The Bruce*, he describes the women of besieged Berwick gathering up bundles of spent English arrows and delivering them to their menfolk on the ramparts.

God's Country

A Highland soldier got into a train travelling to Inverness and sat down beside a Salvation Army officer. He studied the uniform and eventually asked, 'What's your regiment, mon? I canna mak' it oot.' The reply came, 'I'm a soldier of Heaven, I go to Inverness to fight the Devil, then on to Dundee, then Edinburgh and Newcastle, fighting all the time.' Said the Highlander with a knowing nod, 'That's the way – keep heading the bugger sooth.'

Let's Get it Right This Time

Following the comprehensive defeat of the English army at Stirling Bridge in 1297, when the flower of English chivalry was cut down after being trapped on a narrow bridge over the Forth, Edward I, on his campaign of 1303, arranged for pontoon bridges, built at King's Lynn in Norfolk, to be shipped north. This time, his army safely negotiated the river.

Hit Me with the Hyperbole

The great Canadian-born economist J K Galbraith, writing about his upbringing in the Scottish township of Dunwich, Ontario, makes mention of the MacKillop brothers, noted for their red hair and spectacular, wiry red beards. One sorry individual who unwisely swung a punch at one of the MacKillops connected with the Canadian Scot's chin and was left with a lacerated fist 'that looked as if it had been in contact with barbed wire'.

Fighting in the Streets

Warfare between Glasgow gangs, such as the Billy Boys (Prods) and the Norman Conks (Tims), in the 1930s could be almost medieval in its intensity. On a Sunday, the Billy Boys would march into enemy territory with their flute band leading the way. They would be met by an avalanche of buckets of filth, bricks or broken glass from the windows or even roofs of the tenements. Sir Percy Sillitoe, the city's chief constable, said that, if they could have made boiling lead, the gangs would not have hesitated to use that. In his poem 'King Billy', Glasgow's poet laureate Edwin Morgan describes the funeral in the 1960s of a leader of the Protestant Billy Boys and recalls the 'famous sherrickings' of three decades previously.

Writing on the Wall

In the 1960s the graffiti of the Glasgow gangs always included the phrase 'Ya Bas', which most folk took to be an abbreviated bit of foul and abusive language. In fact, it takes its derivation from the rather appropriate Gaelic war cry *Aigh bas* which means 'Battle and die'. Another familiar Glasgow symbol with a surprisingly violent pedigree is the robin on the city's coat-of-arms, which recalls St Kentigern's restoration to life of a bird stoned by a gang of young tykes. Nice to see the sweep of historical continuity.

The Roman Vietnam

Hadrian's Wall was begun in 122 AD on the orders of the Roman Emperor to shut out the troublesome Picts who were responsible for many setbacks to the Roman cause, including the complete disappearance of the Ninth Legion – 6,000 men, who had been sent north to rap Pictish knuckles. As many as 50,000 legionaries and mercenaries are thought to have been killed in three centuries of guerrilla war waged by the tribes.

Who's for the High Jump?

English prisoners held at Borthwick Castle near Gorebridge in Midlothian were given the opportunity to earn their freedom by leaping across a 12-foot gap between the castle's twin towers. The jump had to be made across the 110-foot drop from a standing start with their hands tied behind their backs. How many made it is not recorded.

CHAPTER 4

Houghmagandie an' a Wee Hauf

Claret and Sculduddery

Harlotry Run Riot

Georgian society was rocked in 1796 by a report from a former Lord Provost of Glasgow, Patrick Colquhoun, entitled *A Treatise on the Police of the Metropolis*. On examining crime in London, he suggested the existence of a criminal 'class'. Colquhoun, who was born in Dumbarton, claimed that one in eight people in the whole of London, or 115,000 citizens, were making a living from crime. They included thieves, muggers and forgers, not to mention others, such as scavengers, bear-baiters and gypsies, who were perhaps less obvious members of this huge criminal underclass. So sensational were his findings that the treatise went through five successive annual reprints. Within its pages he also estimated that London was home to 50,000 harlots but this included women who lived with, but were not married to, their partners. As author Rob Hughes has asked – on that basis how many whores would a modern-day Colquhoun find in the metropolis?

By one of these nice twists of history, after completing his study of the great army of London 'harlots', Colquhoun was appointed as British agent for the Caribbean colony of the Virgin Isles.

The Drouthy Bishop of St Andrews

One of the most interesting ecclesiastical rows in medieval Scotland was noted in 1203 when the thirsty bishop of St Andrews rebuked the monks of Dunfermline for being a bit stingy with the claret during an official visit. The monks, in turn, accused the bishop and his team of an over-fondness for drink.

Destination Scotland

Scotland's level of claret consumption in the 1300s was truly staggering for such a small nation. The historian/reporter Froissart, famed for his enormous chronicles, reported that, on one occasion, he saw up to 200 vessels in Gascony, probably at Bordeaux, some as small as 50 tons. All had a consignment of wine and many were heading for Scotland.

At Leith in medieval times, a hogshead of the new wine, recently arrived from France, would be carted around the town and everyone given a chance to sample the vintage at cut-price rates before, hopefully, proceeding to a more substantial purchase.

A Smacker to Remember

Perhaps the most famous screen kiss – that passionate lip-numbing effort in the Honolulu surf – was shared by Burt Lancaster and Helensburgh lass Deborah Kerr, who was born in the Clydeside town in 1921. The film, of course, was *From Here To Eternity*.

By the by, have you heard about the Helensburgh pairing which changed the world? John Logie Baird is unquestionably the Clydeside town's most famous son. However, his breakthrough in the 1920s in perfecting television was due in no small measure to financial help given by Helensburgh-born actor and singer Jack Buchanan at a time when Baird was struggling for development capital.

Well and Truly on the Rocks

During the first winter of the thirteenth century, according to the historian Hector Boece, the weather was so cold that beer froze into lumps and was served by the pound.

It's an interesting side-line that Scotland's two great military defeats took place, in a chillingly appropriate way, with the rain absolutely chucking it down. Downpours were reported at Flodden in September 1513 and Culloden in April 1746.

Was the Cuddy to Blame?

Alexander III, King of Scots, took a fatal heider over the cliffs at Kinghorn in Fife in 1286, throwing the Scottish political scene into chaos. Usually the poor old horse gets the blame for tripping but some experts believe that drink and sex may have been a factor. Alexander, they speculate, may have had a cargo aboard after a drinking session in Edinburgh and was hot to get home for a night of passion in the arms of his new bride, Yolande.

All fur a Wee Swallie

Experts suggest that as much as a third of the annual barley crop in medieval Scotland was destined for brewing. A weak barley beer was our nation's everyday drink of choice.

Wine imports to the Western Isles were restricted in 1622 because it had been noted that the arrival of a vessel carrying wine signalled 'excessive drinking and breaking of His Majesty's Peace'.

In Scotland, by the 1930s, restrictive licensing laws often led to bizarre situations. On Sundays, you had to prove you were a bona fide traveller with at least three miles under your belt before you could get a drink at a hotel. For example, Dollar in Clackmannanshire is three miles from Tillicoultry and, each Sunday, the villages swapped their drinking populations. A double-decker bus would take folk the regulation three miles for a drink, with every passenger carefully grasping the all-important bus ticket – their passport to a wee refreshment.

Cheeky Devil

George Buchanan, scholar and tutor to James VI, once told a fawning and flattering courtier, 'Ye may kiss his arse but I hae skelpit it.'

This is not the only occasion on which the monarch's buttocks reached the annals. When James made his famous journey south in 1603 to take the throne of England, he soon got cheesed off with the adoring mobs. On one occasion, when he complained about this attention, the king was told that the crowd wanted to see as much of him as possible. 'God's wounds,' cursed Jamie, 'then I will pull down my breeches and they shall also see my arse.' Bearing in mind Jamie's flexible sexuality, these anecdotes are of interest.

A Quick Rub Doon wi' a Wet Haddock

There were opportunities not to be missed in Glasgow in 1906 if the newspaper ads are anything to go by. Madame Rosenstein was offering 'German medical rubbing' which, according to reports, was absolutely infallible – in relieving exactly which problems we're not certain. Even more intriguingly, a Miss Carlo was practising 'simple massage' but using the 'Parisian method'. No word yet of seedy saunas.

Janet's Tail Tops Them All

James IV was a regular visitor at the shrine of St Duthac at Tain, in Ross and Cromarty, around the turn of the sixteenth century when pilgrimage was still a popular pursuit of all classes. Whether James's trips north were due to the special sanctity of the place or the fact that, according to royal records, 'Janet Bare-Arse' resided in the village is something we can now only ponder.

Heading for a Fall

Aristotle, admittedly a clever chap, did have some strange ideas about the effects of alcohol. After long, careful and dedicated study, he concluded that those who got drunk on our national drink, whisky, fell over backwards while those who overdid the vino collapso tended to fall flat on their faces. Falling over sideways may be the result of mixing the grain with the grape, but experiments continue.

Whisky, of course, is a noted cure-all. Writing in 1577, historian Raphael Holinshed penned this marvellous piece of PR for the Scotch whisky industry: 'Beying moderately taken, it cutteth fleume, lighte-neth the mynd, quickeneth the spirit, cureth the hydropsie, healeth the stranguary, repelleth gravel, puffeth away ventositie ... and keepeth the head from whirlying ...' No' so sure about that last point.

It is a noteworthy fact that it was 1840 before the first commercially made whisky reached the market place – helped along by the patronage of Queen Victoria. Brewing in early modern Scotland was usually the preserve of the brewster-wife, and the man interfered with this vital work at his peril. Civic records show that, in 1530, there were 288 female brewsters in Edinburgh.

Drawing a Line

Stonehaven's Lord Reith, first General Manager of the British Broadcasting Corporation in 1922 and later Director General, banned the word 'drawers' from programmes because he feared it might promote lusty thoughts.

Transvestites at the Graveside

In 1576, Madge Morison of Aberdeen was fined for the bizarre offence of dressing up in men's clothing at a funeral. It seems that it was a favourite pastime in the Granite City for young folk to swop clothes with members of the opposite sex and parade through the town. How much have things changed in the windy city during the past 400 years? Clearly this was an all-Scottish phenomenon because, two years earlier, Janet Cadie was summoned before the kirk in Edinburgh, accused of disguising herself in 'velvet breikis' and dancing in men's clothing.

It would appear that it was Scotland's pagans who led the way for the rest of the world in the art and sport of cross-dressing. For the Celts, Hallowe'en was an opportunity to try on not only a new persona but a new gender. It's said that the Scotsman's tendency to favour the bare leg always had us ahead in the transvestite stakes.

The Meenisters and the Demon

If you believe the propaganda, then your image of Scotland after the Reformation in 1560 will probably be of a nation lost under a grey cloud of joylessness. Well, you'd be wrong! As late as 1576, the General Assembly was cautioning ministers and elders, who 'tapis ale, beir or wine', or kept an alehouse, that they should conduct their business with all appropriate decorum.

The clergy's interest in drink is nicely illustrated by the story of a church service at Laurencekirk in Kincardineshire in the 1800s. A celebrated resident of the town, a lady who kept the local inn, fell fast asleep in the front pew and, despite the promptings of her neighbours, continued to dose. Eventually the minister, seeing the commotion said, 'Let her alone – I'll soon waken her: Whew, whew, Janet, a bottle o' ale and a dram, if you please.' Janet awoke with a start, declaring, 'Coming richt up, sir!'

Time, Gentlemen, Please!

The idea that early closing might cut rowdiness and street crime has a surprisingly long pedigree. In 1436, the Scots Parliament, meeting in Edinburgh, ordered the closure of all public houses by 9 p.m. under pain of imprisonment.

Café Latte and Biscotti, You Said

In the late 1800s, Scottish temperance reformers had a tee-total paddle steamer, *The Ivanhoe*. It cruised the Clyde in competition with the appropriately named pleasure steamboats, which were often notorious floating pubs and gave the Scottish vernacular the word 'steamin' to describe the behaviour of the seaborne drunken hordes.

In 1852, in an attempt to bring about more sobriety in the northern herring fleet, the Duke of Sutherland offered to replace the whisky entitlement of crews, fishing out of Helmsdale, with a supply of coffee and the equipment for making it. He was not killed in the rush.

We Have a Word for it

For a country where the shadow of Calvin still stalks the streets and 'sex' is something in which they carried the coal to posh houses in Corstorphine or Bearsden, we do have a wheen of fine words to describe the sexual act. My own favourites include the marvellously evocative 'houghmagandie' and the equally enticing 'sculduddery'. A 'dyke-louper' was a loose woman, possibly the mother of an illegitimate child.

Sexy words got Roxburghshire-born poet and nineteenth-century doctor John Armstrong into a spot of bother when he published two worthy but controversial works back-to-back. First came a serious study called *A Synopsis of the History and Care of Venereal Disease*, which he swiftly followed up with a cheeky poem titled 'The Economy of Love', condemned for 'inflaming the passions of youth'.

Water, Water Everywhere

Alcohol has been, and remains, a lethal substance in the wrong hands. In 1664, in a tragic twist on the theme of over-indulgence, the young Earl of Leven died after a serious drinking bout with some gay blades in Edinburgh. He is said to have consumed enormous quantities of seawater while re-crossing the Forth.

Chaste but Never Caught

Bundlin' – a strange tradition which allowed a betrothed couple to share a bed and get to know each other while tightly wrapped in secure clothing to prevent any hanky-panky – was widely practised in the north of Scotland in centuries past. Some chaste individuals even slept with their lower half – their business end, if you like – tied into a pillowcase and others laid a bolster between the couple – a sort of sexual no-go area. Even with such precautions, it's difficult to believe that there weren't regular cross-bolster incursions.

Bonnie Charlie's Fu' as a Wilk

Heavy bevvying by Bonnie Prince Charlie in his later years is traced by some historians to the five months spent in hiding in the Highlands after Culloden. He is said to have regularly enjoyed a dram in his caves and hideaways, in an attempt to keep cold, hunger, fatigue and depression at bay.

Flashing for Beginners

Crime statistics in the hands of the honest Glasgow police officer can be put into some marvellously innocent spins. Witness the Glasgow constable who, when asked in court about the frequency of offences of indecent exposure, said they were common enough in summer but tended to drop off in the winter.

Prepare for a Bit of Brain Strain

West Lothian tailor Alexander Blair was condemned to death in September 1630 for marrying his first wife's half-brother's daughter – incest in the confused eyes of the law in Scotland. This is complex enough but other such cases I've encountered come into the category of the truly mind-boggling. A century later in Ayrshire, a case was heard which one contemporary commentator declared was 'capable of being stated in words but calculated to rack the brain of whoever tried to realise its conception'. Let's try – John M'Taggart married a woman named Janet Kennedy whose former husband Anthony McHarg was a brother to M'Taggart's grandmother (still with us?), who, in turn, was said to have been the natural daughter of Anthony McHarg's father. Hold it – I feel a migraine coming on!

Now, Gentlemen, to Clause 1406 . . .

Patrick Ruthven, Earl of Forth, who distinguished himself in the service of the Swedish king Gustavus Adolphus in the early 1600s, was valued not only for his bravery on the battlefield but also as a diplomatic negotiator. On his CV was a recommendation which must have served him well through the long nights at the conference table: 'He could drink immeasurably and preserve his understanding to the last.'

The Foul Pox Puts in an Appearance

The English called it 'The French Disease', the French called it 'The Neapolitan Disease', the Neapolitans called it 'The Spanish Disease'. . . nobody but nobody would accept responsibility for syphilis which, according to some scholars, may have reached Europe with the returning expedition of Christopher Columbus in the late 1400s. It's a wonder the rest of Europe didn't blame it on the Irish or the Scots, who were too often charged with responsibility for Europe's ills.

We have to admit, however, that it reached Scotland quite rapidly. In 1497, during the reign of James IV, a statute ordered all sufferers to be banished to the island of Inchkeith in the River Forth. Many famous Scots are said to have suffered from this 'foul pox', including Mary Queen of Scots' husband, Lord Henry Darnley.

Predictions (Mainly Misguided)

In 1923, the Anti-Saloon League, which sounds as if it probably had its roots in Dodge City, forecast at a meeting in Glasgow that Scotland would be a 'dry' nation within ten years. Another interesting example of forecasting in relation to drink was the occasion when a new bishop was appointed in Orkney. By tradition, he drank from the cup of St Magnus and the amount he was able to get over his neck in a oner was said to indicate the likely length of his tenure.

Discreet Concubine-Keeping

Among the statutes ordered in the mid-1400s by Bishop Kennedy for St Salvator's College at St Andrews, we find that students were warned against keeping concubines or acting like common nightwalkers or robbers. And what were the scholars studying? Divinity, of course. A wee reformation needed there, perhaps?

A Touch Too Much

The health-giving properties of the water from St Corbet's Well in the Touch Hills near Stirling were withdrawn by the saint, according to legend, after boisterous May Day revellers turned the annual pilgrimage to the magic waters into a glorious booze-up.

Out Among the Silver Darlings

In the 1840s at Wick, an incredible fleet gathered for the annual herring fishery. In the first year of the decade, it was reported that 428 local boats and 337 from further afield were operating out of the port and the local minister loudly complained that, when the fleet was in, Wick was drinking up to 500 gallons of whisky in a day. Twentieth-century novelist Neil Gunn wrote of those self-same crews, recalling how, as they hauled in their nets, they began to sing, one after another, a Psalm of David until it seemed that the sea itself sang. If you think that's impressive, you should have heard them later that day in the pub!

A Rose by Any Other Name

Romantics among us have always believed that Edinburgh's Rose Street was named after the bushes of wild roses which decorated the slopes above the Nor' Loch (now Waverley Station) in the days before the construction of the New Town. Silly, sugary dumplings that we are! Many European towns have their very own Rose Street because it is commonly used to describe the 'red light' district and to 'pluck a rose' was a common euphemism for 'copulating with a prostitute'. Further north, although Aberdeen took on the appearance of a frontier town during the oil boom of the 1970s, we discover that it had been preparing the way for more than a century. Official police records show that, in 1857, there were 34 brothels in the Granite City. And, in the depths of the Industrial Revolution, the sixteenth of a square mile around Glasgow's Saltmarket was reckoned to be one of the most corrupt locations in Europe. It 'boasted' 150 shebeens, or illegal drinking dens, and an amazing total of 200 brothels.

Frontier Refreshments

The Scottish heritage in the United States can take some unusual forms. In the early 1900s, archaeologists, working at Fort Apache in Arizona, uncovered stone bottles that had been imported from Edinburgh and which once contained McEwen's ale. Mind you, an empty bottle of whisky is said to have been found under Hitler's bed in his Berlin bunker in 1945 and, as far as we know, the Führer had no strong Scottish connections.

You'll Have Had Your Tea?

Tea is said to have been first introduced to polite Scottish society in 1687 by Mary of Modena, wife of the Stuart king, James VII. She brought along a caddy to a meeting of the General Assembly of the Church of Scotland. The ministers were not impressed and initially Scotland's males shunned the drink as a 'improper innovation' liable to render the population 'weak and effeminate'. The new beverage did cause confusion, however, when it first arrived in Scotland in quantity in the early 1700s. Some society women, unaware of how exactly to serve this new luxury, occasionally put it on a slice of bread and butter.

The Edinburgh greeting, 'You'll have had your tea?', seen – at least by Glaswegians – to denote the icy hospitality generally to be found in the capital, is said to have originated with a nobleman – Mackintosh of Borlum – who, in 1729, complained of this widespread and evergrowing habit of tea slurping. When out visiting friends, he had to confirm that he had already had his tea so that he could receive the more traditional glass of beer.

Someone else who worried about the new fashion was Duncan Forbes of Culloden, the Lord President of the Court of Session, who enjoyed a glass of whisky and was so concerned about the growing use of tea that he campaigned to have its consumption restricted to the working classes. It is certainly true that tea subsequently became a drink of the people. During the Radical Unrest of the 1820s, a group of weavers' wives in Paisley decided to make a major sacrifice and renounce tea-drinking because of its excise duty. With full ceremony they carried their teapots to the nearby bridge and threw them into the river. It's said that the anti-tea-drinking vow was later ratified with many glasses of smuggled whisky.

Mummy's Boy

Sir Thomas Lipton (1850–1931), Glasgow's very own tea tycoon, gifted £10,000 to his native city of Glasgow for the relief of poor mothers and children – in memory of his own mother. Apparently, one of her biggest problems had been that she didn't know how to make a decent cup o' tea and this set Thomas on his career. Ironic, eh?

Sipping the Light Fantastic

Whisky was not widely consumed in Scotland much before the 1800s. Home-brewed ale was supped in enormous quantities, as was imported wine, particularly from Bordeaux. However, today, our cratur is the envy of the world. Old Havana is not, as you might imagine, a brand of cigar but is, in fact, Cuba's own malt whisky. The received wisdom is that Cubans gathered the formula on an industrial espionage mission for Fidel Castro in the 1980s. The bearded freedom fighter – like most of the rest of the world, it seems – claims a Scottish heritage.

It's a Sin, so it Is!

Perhaps the hardest news for whisky drinkers to swallow is that, during its production process, whisky evaporates up Scottish distillery lums at a terrifying rate equivalent to 150 million bottles annually. From my years as a reporter in the distilling town of Dumbarton, I can confirm that the aroma was thick in the air most days and a walk down the High Street could often be achieved without your feet ever touching the pavement.

Cheers Yersel!

Whisky is used to toast everything from the New Year to new babies, from Robbie Burns to the all too infrequent Scottish successes on the sporting field. But did you know that the cratur has a toast all of its own? It runs something like this: 'Here's to whisky – as old as a grown man, as wild as goat's milk, as soothing as a lover's hand through your hair and as inspiring as Robbie Shepherd's Reel Blend!'

Dope on a Rope

In the warmer summers of medieval Scotland, cannabis was grown widely as hemp for rope-making to supply the nation's ever-expanding merchant fleet. Hence the phrase, I imagine, 'Draggin' on a rope'.

The Boys Are Back in Town

When a papal delegate was travelling through the north of England in the mid 1400s, word came of an imminent attack by a wild band of Scots Border reivers. The men in the nearby villages took to their heels but, according to the churchman, the women refused to scarper 'for they had no fear that the enemy would do them evil' – not reckoning violation to be an evil.

Scottish Underwear – a Brief History

One of the great scandals of the Church of Scotland in the late 1600s concerned the Rev. John McQueen, an Edinburgh minister who was so besotted with a local beauty, Mrs Euphame Scott, that he stole pieces of her undergarments from the washing line. Nothing spectacularly unusual there, you might think. But the hot and bothered reverend gentleman went a step further. From Mrs Scott's unmentionables he made a waistcoat and drawers, having been convinced by some old High Street charmer, no doubt, that this unusual bit of tailoring would magically and inexorably draw her to him. As far as we know, it did not work.

A Few Knick-Knacks

Star item at the Scottish Tartans Museum in Keith is not, as you might expect, their piece of plaid dated 325 AD but a pair of underpants – woolly drawers – in the stunning Royal Stewart tartan, which belonged to Queen Victoria's gillie and boyfriend – possibly husband? – John Brown.

Swashbuckling John Paul Jones, founder of the United States Navy, who also served in the French and Russian navies, was born at Arbigland in Kircudbrightshire in 1747. One of his less familiar claims to fame is that he achieved most of his notable victories beneath the petticoats of the ladies of New England. His vessel carried a national flag that had been sewn for him by the young women of Portsmouth, New Hampshire – from their own undergarments.

The presence of thousands of American servicemen in Scotland during the Second World War is said to have had a hypnotic effect on the Scots lasses. On the topic of girls' knickers, one of the most popular jibes was, 'One Yank and they're off!' It is thought that 80,000 American service personnel eventually tied the knot with their British sweethearts.

In April 1929, the latest corset designs went on display at mannequin parades in big city stores in Glasgow. As the girls strutted their twenties stuff on the catwalk, they were accompanied by solos from Miss Ethel Fenton, the celebrated London contralto.

Who says folk were deprived in the pre-television era?

Step we Gaily

One of the biggest attractions for English visitors to Clydeside in the eighteenth century was Glasgow Green where hundreds of girls tramped their washing in tubs with their dresses and petticoats howked up, displaying ample lengths of well-muscled, milky-white thigh. 'Scotch Washing' was finally condemned by prudish Victorians and made redundant by the arrival of 'steamies' or wash-houses.

That's how tae Sell Books!

The first edition of the *Encyclopaedia Britannica*, the brainwave of three Edinburgh men, caused controversy, particularly in the anatomy section, which contained 'unvarnished portrayals of the unmentionable parts of the human body'. Nothing like a good bit of PR to get people interested.

Where's Yer Madonna noo?

If you think that the adoration of musical superstars is a feature of the modern era, then think again. For example, in 1858, singer Blanche Cole appeared at Glasgow's Merchant Hall and her version of 'The Hundred Pipers' had 'the audience carried almost beyond the bounds of concert hall etiquette', according to reviews. A Victorian 'haud-me-back' situation, forsooth.

Too Much Fun and Games

One cause of tremendous indignation among Scottish Reformers in the 1560s were the jollifications and sillibrations at the court of Mary Queen of Scots. Most serious frivolity, according to the greybeards, was the habit of the queen and her ladies of dressing up in male attire for balls and masquerades. Something imported by those damn Frenchies, I'll bet!

Ringing the Changes

When local aristo Lady Janet Anstruther wanted to go for a swim from her summer tower at Sauchar Bay in the East Neuk of Fife, she would send a bellringer round the toon to warn the locals not tae keek. Another theory is that she was a bit of an exhibitionist and was actually trying to attract an audience.

CHAPTER 5

Jock Tamson's Bairns and Bampots

Public and Private Behaviour

The Queen Mary Handicap Chase

The first record of a horse race approximating to a steeplechase goes back to the war-torn 1570s. In a remarkable 18-mile pursuit from Bathgate to Edinburgh, Roger Hepburn – in the Queen's colours – cleared dykes and ditches on his 'old nag' to outstrip his bloodthirsty pursuers, enemies of Mary, and gain sanctuary in the castle.

Scotland claims to have one of the oldest genuine horse races in the world – the Marymass event at Irvine – which is thought to have first been run in the 1100s. Betting was always a part of the Scottish race scene but, in the seventeenth century, any sum over 100 merks won at the gee-gees had to be given to the poor.

Working up a Sweat

In the Western Isles, a primitive form of sauna was used to sweat an illness from a patient. A fierce fire was set on an earthen floor and, when the floor was heated, the fire was removed, hay placed on the earth and water poured on the patient before he or she was placed on the straw, 'putting the whole body in a sweat'. A case of the cure being more alarming than the illness, perhaps.

Another novel way of working up a sweat was reported in Lewis at the end of the Second World War. Senior officers in the Highland constabulary were concerned about the amount of time constables were spending chasing runaway sheep around the back streets of Stornoway.

Luigi's Palace of Many Pleasures

What could be nicer on a warm summer Sunday afternoon than popping into a café for an ice cream. Well, in 1911, the United Free Church sought amendments to the Shops Bill which would ban ice-cream sales on a Sunday. Their anxiety stemmed from a report by the

Inspector of the Poor for Glasgow, who was a worried man. Ice-cream shops, he declared, had a bad record for the seduction of young girls, 'because of temptations offered therein'. And, just to put the tin lid on it, he reckoned there might be as many as 17,000 women in Glasgow living an 'immoral' life. And here was me just looking for a pokey hat and a slider!

Enforced Silence

A popular Scottish punishment used by the magistrates in the Borders against gossips and scandalmongers was the 'branks' – a headpiece with an iron bar which was jammed in the mouth trapping the tongue and preventing speech. In a more sinister use, it was also brought into play during the questioning of suspected witches.

Bring the Needle North

Local enthusiasts claim that one of the most famous London land-marks, the 186-ton Cleopatra's Needle on the Thames Embankment, should be relocated in its spiritual home – not by the banks of the Nile, but in Bridge of Allan. They argue that Sir James Alexander, who transported the pink granite obelisk from Egypt in 1867, always intended that it should be displayed in a public park in the Stirlingshire town.

One Palace Going Cheap

Scotland's greatest conman – a title for which there are surely a wheen of contenders – was probably actor Arthur Fergusson who, in the 1920s, set himself up in the business of selling off some of Britain's most famous monuments. He disposed of Nelson's Column, Buckingham Palace and Big Ben to gullible Americans and was eventually jailed Stateside after persuading an Australian (with corks in his bunnet, sans doute) to buy the Statue of Liberty.

In the annals of Scottish crime, there are recorded many strange, outlandish – even uncanny – offences. In recent times, a man was jailed for six months at Hamilton for various offences, including slicing the blue flashing light off a police patrol car with an Indian Army cavalry sword.

Gie's Oor Stone Back!

When the Stone of Destiny was 'retrieved' for the nation from Westminster Abbey on Christmas Day 1950 by a group of young Scots, it prompted a huge police operation. Such was the constitutional alarm at this audacious theft that, for the first time in four centuries, the border between Scotland and England was completely closed.

Serious Intent

The resolve of the early postal service in Scotland to get the job done is illustrated by an advert for the new Edinburgh–Inverness service in 1669. It defiantly stated, 'A waggon will leave the Grassmarket for Inverness every Tuesday, God willing, but on Wednesday, whether or no!'

Tenement Torture

A tried and trusted, yet mean and nasty, technique for clearing the ubiquitous street singers from Glasgow's backcourts was to lob red hot pennies from the tenement window and watch the poor strolling players burn their fingers in attempting to pick them up. Of course, the smart singers learned to use their bunnets to collect the red hot coinage.

What About the Long Johns?

In 1289, in a special dispensation approved by Pope Nicholas IV in person, the monks of Lindores in Fife were given permission to break a centuries-old tradition and wear caps as protection against the kingdom's icy blasts (Fife's, not Heaven's).

Samba through the Street

Long before South American footballers became ten a penny on Scottish pitches, a Brazilian played briefly for Clydebank FC in the 1960s. He did not adapt well to the harsher aspects of the Scottish climate. On one famous occasion, the South American was taken from the park suffering from exposure and hypothermia during a league match on a wild, winter's afternoon at Station Park, Forfar – rather too many miles from the warm sand of Copacabana beach.

Arena of Damaged Pride

Scotland's most famous duelling arena was the grassy slope below Arthur's Seat in Edinburgh. The last-known duel fought there involved a Court of Session judge Lord Shand in 1850, with again, as often happened, the only injuries sustained being damaged pride. Kirkcaldy in Fife has a claim to the last 'genuine' duel rather than a social skirmish. This is said to have taken place in 1826 between two business men.

One 'Fuck' Too Many

Twentieth-century Glasgow dramatist James Bridie (Osborne Henry Mavor) was of the opinion that few languages could equal Scots in its range of terms of abuse. For starters he cited: 'thowless, blowtering nyaffs, feckless, donnart, doited, havering gowks; daft, glaikit foutering taupies and snuitet gomerals'. Now that 'fuck' is used as a boring, repetitive, everyday expletive, particularly by younger folk, it may be time to return to this rich Scots vein of verbal assault.

The Protector's Proboscis

Crowds lined the streets of Edinburgh in 1650 to see the spectacular arrival of Oliver Cromwell, victor of the Battle of Dunbar, in the Scottish capital. And what was the abiding memory of that historic day for the citizens? Was it the pomp and pageantry, the military might of the Parliamentary army which had dealt so decisively with the Covenanters? No, the lasting recollection, the talking point in the hostelries along the High Street and down the Grassmarket for weeks afterwards was the size of the Lord Protector's nose. Oliver's snout stole the show!

The Season to Be Merry

One of the most serious public disturbances in Edinburgh during the Victorian period was the notorious two-day snowball riot which raged around the university and the South Bridge in January 1838. Eventually the military were called out from the castle to support the police in the battle between students and citizens. The Riot Act was read and police stormed into the Quadrangle to arrest the student scrappers who had sought sanctuary on the university campus. The university authorities objected to this intrusion on their jurisdiction and, although the students were eventually let off without punishment, gates were erected at the entrance to the Old Quad, not to keep the students in but to keep the police out!

Chowing Over an Accent

An Ayrshire servant lass who spoke with the broadest dialect returned from London with a pronounced English accent. Asked how she had learned this so easily, she reverted – to the immense relief of her pals – to her Ayrshire speak. 'Och it's easy eneuch. A' ye've got tae dae is just to leave oot the Hs and Rs and gie the words a bit chow in the middle.'

That Wild Dunoon Mob

Councillors at Dunoon decided in 1898 that, although the real world was beginning to close in around them, they would not open the pier to steamers from Glasgow on Sundays. There was a serious track record of civic unrest in relation to previous Sunday visits by the steamers. One councillor reminded his colleagues of the disgraceful scenes on the previous occasion as young men – Bibles in hand and just out of the church – ran happily to meet the steamer and young women – throwing all moral decency oot the windae – brazenly waved handkerchiefs.

Something to Shout About?

At least 15 US presidents had Scottish roots according to experts and it is generally accepted that the number of Scots and Scots descendants among the vice-presidents, congressmen, senators and governors must run into several hundred. Should we trumpet this fact from the rooftops or quietly shove it up a close? Answers on a green card, please.

Anti-Social – Whit, Me?

That classic American frontiersman, Daniel Boone – like Davy Crockett – had Scots blood coursing through his veins. Despite his life on the edge, Boone defied all predictions and lived to a ripe old age, having been married for 57 years. He was obliged to leave school early after putting a laxative in his teacher's hidden bottle of whisky. He enjoyed the company of his tough fellow frontiersmen but valued the solitude of the backwoods in the Carolinas, Kentucky and Missouri. On one occasion he stunned his wife by declaring that they would have to move house because someone had settled rather too close for comfort – 70 miles from the Boone homestead!

Paddling wi' the Reine d'Écosse

When Mary Queen of Scots went for a barefoot paddle in the North Sea while visiting Coldingham Priory in the 1560s, this daring piece of leisure activity was the talk of the steamie for months thereafter.

The Importance of Level-Headedness

Patients entering Craig Dunain psychiatric hospital in Inverness, which closed in the year 2000, were always confused and sometimes alarmed by a sign near the entrance which read, 'Mind Your Head!' In passing, it's worth noting that the world's first training course in psychiatric nursing was inaugurated at the Crichton Royal Hospital in Dumfries in 1854.

In at the Deep End

Insanity was curable, according to our antecedents, if you took the sufferer to St Fillan's Chapel in Perthshire where they would be plunged into an adjacent pool, tumbled about roughly and left to dry out overnight with a holy bell on their head in the draughty chapel. How many people were brought to their senses – and how many died of a chill – is not recorded.

An Orcadian Way with Words

'Reports of my death are greatly exaggerated,' said Mark Twain famously. But, in the early 1900s, when William 'Skatehorn' Laughton, a well-known Orkney eccentric, learned that the local paper had reported his death, he went one better than Twain, stating, 'I saw the report – but I didn't believe it.'

It was also in Orkney that a missing fisherman, having swum for hours to reach the safety of the shore, was greeted by a crofter with the immortal words, 'Were you the man who droon'd this efternoon?'

The Wild Bunch Hit Town

In the 1830s the town of Airdrie (population then 12,500) attracted thousands of hard-drinking, tough-fighting miners from the surrounding coalfields on pay nights. One government official deplored the 'habits of the demoralised' in what bore all the hallmarks of a wild frontier town. Long before the days of the Wild West, there seem to have been eerily familiar problems in the region. In the late 1550s pack trains passing through the uplands of Clydesdale, carrying lead from the Lanarkshire mines to Leith, were reported to be suffering regular attacks from 'the broken men of the Borders'. Mind you, society dinners could also be pretty rowdy. Swearing and drunkenness among the so-called respectable classes seem to have been commonplace in eighteenth-century Scotland – so much so that Lord Braxfield is reported to have apologised for cursing at a lady for poor play during a game of whist. His excuse was that he had mistaken her for his wife!

A Timely Return

Edinburgh's plague legends are plentiful, but the naming of Morocco's Land in the city's Canongate is surely one of the most colourful. The building, with its unusual carved figure of a turbaned Moor, commemorates Andrew Gray who fled from justice, returning in 1645 with a party of Barbary pirates, having made his fortune in the service of the Sultan of Morocco. Using Arabic techniques he is reputed to have cured his cousin, the Provost's daughter, of plague, married her and settled again in his homeland. A film script just waiting to be written? Possible title: *From the Casbah to the Canongate.*

Fever in Fife

The Lomond Hills in Fife witnessed an amazing 'Fool's Gold Rush' in 1847 when hundreds of prospectors set up their encampments, before the adventurers could be convinced that all they were digging up was iron pyrites. Sadly, no goldfield poet was around to record the event as Glasgow bank clerk Robert Service did in the Yukon.

Writing on the Wall

Caledonian graffiti has an ancient pedigree – Viking raiders even scrawled cheeky comments about the Orkney lasses on the walls of the cairn at Maes Howe. Scottish graffiti has been found all over the world, from the sandstone bluffs along the Oregon Trail to the catacombs of Rome, where a message, 'The Scots Were Here, 1447', was found scrawled on a wall. You'll even find some couthy Biblical quotations behind the door of the chapel at the magnificent chateau of Chenonceaux on the Loire, inscribed by a couple of Scots mercenaries in the sixteenth century.

Evidence that defacing public buildings has a long pedigree comes in the 1852 report of two Glasgow boys receiving 12 lashes for chalking obscene words on walls in the East End of the city. I'm willing to bet that curtailed their artistic activity for a wee while.

After painstaking research undertaken from the top deck of buses and in public facilities in the great cities of our land, I can reveal that, apart from the centuries-old pastime of slagging off our English cousins, the most subtle piece of graffiti I've encountered reads, 'If you feel strongly about graffiti, sign a partition'.

A Lame Excuse

Nineteenth-century Poor Law applications – the modern equivalent of social security – can make depressing reading. Among the applications for money from the parish found in Glasgow's records is a plea from a poor soul for cash to allow him to reclaim his wooden leg from the pawnshop.

Tidiness is Next to Godliness

One of the most gifted men of his generation, the Rev. Thomas Chalmers – who led the breakaway from the Church of Scotland to create the Free Church – was a preacher, moral philosopher, mathematician and economist. But, above all, he was fascinated with the intricacies of day-to-day living. Every minute of the day was filled with the exploration of new ideas and concepts and, in one piece of correspondence, he writes with great pride of having invented a new technique of folding his coat which he thought would be of immense value to the traveller. Time for a wee lie down, Tam!

Step Forward the Burntisland Bints

An early example of what appears to be Scotswomen acting in unison in pursuit of truth and justice in what was essentially a man's world came in 1615 when eviction notices were to be served in a Fife burgh. What is described as 'an extraordinary riot' took place in Burntisland when upwards of 100 women of the 'bangster Amazon kind' rioted and 'maist uncourteously dung the officer and his witness aff their feet' when they attempted to read the proclamation. Town magistrates looked on without interfering and, more interestingly, a bailie's wife was said to have been the leader of this tumultuous army. Contemporary observers were in no doubt that the male inhabitants of the town were the instigators. The depressing conclusion is that the women were down-trodden, unsung, oppressed – and exploited.

Chip off the Old Block

In 1857, as Madeleine Smith was being freed in Edinburgh after the controversial charge of poisoning her lover had been found not proven, souvenir hunters were chipping bits of stonework from her house in Glasgow's Blythswood Square. Now you know the origin of that big lump of masonry on the mantelpiece of which grandfaither was so protective.

Loose Breeks Advised

At Ballater on Royal Deeside there is an annual ferret festival, the highlight of which is a competition which involves sliding the 'futtret doon yer troosers' so that the beastie emerges at your feet in the shortest possible time.

Hey, Davie, Haud the Ba'

David II didn't win many friends when, in 1363, he stunned the Scottish Parliament at Scone by suggesting that, if he died without issue, an English prince should be chosen as their sovereign. The explanation for this daft, unpatriotic behaviour was that he was brought up in captivity south of the Border.

Daft as a Hairbrush

In his biographies, Kincardineshire's James Burnett, Lord Monboddo (1714–99), is described as a judge, pioneer anthropologist and eccentric. The truth is that he was one of the most astonishing and imaginative individuals of his generation. It was Monboddo, a widely respected legal figure, who believed that all babies were born with tails and that midwives cut them off as part of some great, unspecific world conspiracy. We laugh now, of course, but in this speculation he anticipated the work of Charles Darwin. Interestingly, a regular medieval taunt by Scottish soldiers when confronted by their English adversaries related to a belief that all English folk were born with tails – it would be fair to say we've been trying to make monkeys out of them ever since.

Monboddo abhorred innovation or modernism of any kind and, when that cutting-edge piece of transport engineering, the sedan chair, reached Edinburgh, he was distinctly underwhelmed. Of course, soon all the top families in the capital had a chair but, to emphasise his disdain, Monboddo would, after a day in court, send his official wig home in style through the streets of Edinburgh in his sedan chair while the noble lord trotted alongside for exercise.

The Long Man

After his wedding to Mary Queen of Scots in 1565, Lord Henry Darnley, with a team of courtiers and hingers-on, strode up and down Edinburgh's High Street, loudly bragging that he had returned Scotland to the Catholic faith. Hooray Henry's moment in the sun was short-lived. He was permanently silenced two years later in the spectacular assassination at Kirk o' Field. Mary Queen of Scots, on seeing her future husband Henry for the first time, remarked that he was the 'best proportioned long man' she had ever seen. On the other hand, Darnley's uncle seemed a bit nearer the mark when he described Darnley as a 'peasant twit'.

The Flute and Whistle's Debut

Partick Thistle FC, the legendary Maryhill Magyars, played their first matches in 1876 on public ground that is now the site of Glasgow's Art Galleries at Kelvingrove. Despite a recent return to the big-time, critics say the team's performances can have a quality of still-life about them yet.

Thanks Be to the Plague

The survival of the bulk of fifteenth-century Scottish poetry from the pens of Dunbar and Henryson and sic' like makars is largely down to successful Edinburgh merchant George Bannatyne (1545–1608) who, when plague raged in the capital in 1568, retired to his family home in Forfarshire where he spent his days copying from the texts of his favourite poets. One of these great poetic masters, Henryson, seems to have had a sense of humour to the last. As he was dying from flux (diarrhoea), a 'wise' woman was brought to the house who told him he would be cured if he walked three times around a particular tree in his orchard repeating the rhyme, 'Whikey tree, whikey tree, take away this flux from me.' Henryson, with a glint in his sceptical academic's eye even at the end, declared he was too weak to perform this ritual and suggested instead that he should go round his bedroom table chanting, 'Oaken burd, Oaken burd, Gar me shit a good hard turd!'

Some State of Ship

In August 1594 the main attraction at the baptism feast of Prince Henry, son of James VI, in the Great Hall at Stirling Castle, was a huge, 40 foot-high mock-up of a ship of state, powered by a hidden crew of 20. Bedecked in gold and red flags and equipped with miniature brass cannon, it 'sailed' down the hall with its seafood cargo of lobster, herring, whiting and crab, all modelled in sugar.

Party Time

In the absence of the electronic entertainment of the twentieth-century, our Scottish ancestors took every opportunity to enjoy a victory celebration. For example, in 1665, when news reached Edinburgh of a great naval victory over the Dutch off Lowestoft (hardly a local success you might say), bonfires were lit, bells rung, cannon fired and 'lupin for joy' was reported in the streets.

CHAPTER 6

Christ, Man, Ye'r in a Bad Way!

Death, Despair, Failures and Flops

The Road and the Miles

When the Government ordered Field Marshall George Wade to carry out a programme which involved building hundreds of miles of road and 42 bridges in the Highlands between 1725 and 1738, the project was designed to curb the Jacobite threat following the 1715 uprising and to symbolise London's authority. The idea was that the new highways would get government troops more rapidly to any troublespots. During the '45, however, most British troops were off fighting on the Continent. It is perhaps one of the great ironies of the Jacobite era that the people who got most value out of this splendid network of roads and bridges were Bonnie Prince Charlie and his wee tartan army on their way to Edinburgh and points south.

The other interest groups who were eternally grateful to 'Geordie the Roadman' were Scotland's whisky smugglers and cattle drovers. In fact, although Wade is always the man associated with the construction of the roads, his successor, an officer/engineer called William Caulfield, built some 750 miles – more than three times Wade's total. These included the Stirling–Fort William route through Glencoe (93 miles).

Wrapped up in a Legend

When Flora Macdonald, famed for helping to speed Bonnie Prince Charlie to exile after the Battle of Culloden, died in March 1790, a sheet in which the Prince had slept was used as her shroud.

For Whom the Bell Tolls

Bishop Robert Leighton, an Edinburgh-born cleric, had often said he would like to die in a public house. Friends and family, quite naturally, treated this as a mild eccentricity but, unlike most folk, the prelate got his wish, passing over in The Bell, in London's Warwick Lane in 1684.

Signalling Departure

They say that death is the great leveller – but is it? In the Northern Isles, a funeral procession was formerly preceded by the kirk officer ringing a handbell – a big clanger for the wealthy and a wee ting-a-ling for the poor.

In Defense of Linen

Scots tended to be quick to defend their textile industry. In 1696, in an effort to promote the making of linen, it was forbidden to bury corpses in anything but plain linen and relatives had to take an oath to that effect.

Rushing to Eternity

On her long rail trips to and from Balmoral, Queen Victoria, who detested speeding, never allowed the royal train to travel at more than 40 m.p.h. Ironically her last journey by rail – on board her funeral train through the south of England – was completed at speeds of up to 80 m.p.h. because of late running.

Ominous Omission

It was once the custom in Scotland for the 'guid richt hand' to be excluded from actual dooking during the ceremony of baptism because it would certainly be used in years ahead for killing.

Shoddy Clockmanship

In the early 1500s, Aberdeen's town clock, or 'horologe', on the Tolbooth had clunked to a halt and the town could not apparently provide a mechanic skilled enough to repair it. The clock was packed up and sent to Flanders for repair but was returned after a year 'not much improved'.

The Indignity of Office

The image we get of Scots royalty is not always one of pomp and majesty. For example, in 1593, the Earl of Bothwell and his cronies, anxious to get back into favour with James VI, came in at the back gate to Holyrood Palace early one morning. A naturally apprehensive James, roused from his slumbers, gave them an audience – with, according to the annals, 'his breeks in his hand'.

Beware the Iced Lemonade

Fife-born minister's son Sir David Wilkie – whose paintings of rustic Scottish scenes, such as *The Blind Fiddler* and *Pitlessie Fair*, made him internationally renowned – died on his way home from an artistic expedition in the Holy Land in 1841, from an illness brought on by an over-consumption of iced lemonade and fruit.

No Redeeming Qualities?

Sometimes we like to kid ourselves that the whole world loves Scotland and the Scots. In fact, there have been many who have taken a genuine scunner to the sons and daughters of Caledonia, difficult though this may be to believe. In the mid 1800s a commentary on the Scots inhabiting the Pictou district of Nova Scotia in Canada declared they were 'a canting, covenanting, oat-eating, money gripping tribe of second-hand Scotch Presbyterians: a transplanted, degenerate, barren patch of high cheek-bones and red hair with nothing cleaving them to the original stock except covetousness'. Red-haired – whit, us?

How Dare They?

The myth of Scottish meanness lingers for no good reason. Most recently I saw an American definition of centrifrugal force – the strong inward force experienced by a unit of currency clasped in the hand of a rapidly rotating Scotsman. It's time this piece of nonsense was laid to rest.

Knowing Your Place

Lepers in Scotland were generously allowed to beg in the streets as long as they obeyed two important guidelines – their mouths had to covered at all times and they had to walk in the gutter.

The Mackerel of St Monance

The bell in the old kirk at St Monance in Fife used to hang from a tree but was removed during the herring season because the villagers believed its distinctive clang terrified the fish and chased them out of the estuary.

Rocket Mail is Put on Hold

The Hebridean island of Scarp was the venue in 1934 for a historic experiment – sending mail by rocket to the nearby mainland. Unfortunately the rocket – designed by a German engineer – exploded on take-off and the few surviving letters, with three halfpence stamps and distinctive postmarks, are now collector's items.

Dragonhide Bob

Robert Dreghorn, a wealthy nineteenth-century Glasgow bachelor nicknamed Bob Dragon, was widely regarded as the most ugly man of his generation. According to writer Margaret Thomson Davis, he was 'tall and gaunt, an inward bend in his back and enormous head with one blind eye and one squint eye'. As if that wasn't enough, he had a Roman nose twisted until it lay nearly flat on his cheek. But I'll bet his mammy loved him!

Too Much Information

School history is now most often a series of projects and presentations but, in years past, the avalanche of dates and legions of personalities could be a confusing business for the sair-pressed pupil. One youngster made what can only be described as a perfectly natural mix-up between King Robert Bruce and King Alfred when he described the great Scottish victory in 1314 as the Battle of Bannocks Burnt!

A Wee Corner of New Scotland

During the creation of the so-called Nova Scotia baronets in 1624 and an attempt to promote settlement, the esplanade at Edinburgh Castle was declared to be an integral, legal part of the Atlantic edge of Canada. This was done to allow the baronets to claim their territory in the accepted manner by setting their buckled shoes on officially designated Canadian land but making the dangerous and uncomfortable sea journey unnecessary.

Sir Robert Gordon was the first of these so-called Nova Scotia baronets under Sir William Alexander of Menstrie's plan to create a Scots colony. Sir Bob argued strongly in favour of calling the island colony New Galloway, after the royal burgh just down the road from his castle, but Sir William's proud Latin designation of Nova Scotia won the day.

A Difficult Case to Argue

That arch-villain Lord Robert Stewart – half-brother of Mary Queen of Scots and despotic head of a cruel dynasty which ran Orkney as its personal kingdom – changed the laws of the land to suit his own purposes. As the Orkney-based writer Eric Linklater reported, Stewart even resorted to the ingenious device of accusing dead men of old crimes, then confiscated what property their families had left.

A Classic Thumbs-Down

Edinburgh's Alexander Graham Bell (1847–1922), who developed the first practical telephone while working on the development of hearing aids, was given no encouragement at all when he first introduced his invention to the world. Western Union declared, after a demonstration, that the telephone was 'an interesting novelty without any commercial possibilities'. Bell, it goes without saying, got the last laugh. His patent for the telephone became the single most valuable in history. There is a strange, unverifiable story told of his burial in Nova Scotia. While the service was under way, it's said that every telephone in North America fell silent in tribute.

A Shocking Suggestion

In the early 1800s it was still possible for a judge to order the body of an executed criminal to be dissected by a professor of anatomy for the benefit of medical students. A probably apocryphal but entertaining story connected with this practice involved a man who was strung up at Glasgow Green in 1818 and taken up the road to the University of Glasgow. By way of experiment, a galvanic shock was applied to the deceased, who immediately sat up. The professor, seeing all sorts of problems and inquiries, acted promptly. He took a scalpel and cut the patient's throat. The man is said to have dropped to the floor like a slaughtered ox.

Standing-Room Only

The best-attended lecture in the history of Edinburgh's medical school came in 1829 when the body of William Burke, the murderer who had supplied the school with corpses for dissection, was himself laid out and put to the knife a few hours after his execution. By all accounts, the students were hanging from the rafters for the event.

Bring oot Yer Deid

The last recorded outbreak of bubonic plague in Scotland took place in Glasgow during the early months of the twentieth century. Of 48 diagnosed cases, 16 people died. The filthy state of the city's docklands and the unacceptable number of rats were identified as the causes. The tranquil island of Inchcolm in the River Forth, just off Aberdour in Fife was used as a plague station. In 1580, the records tell us that a ship carrying Edinburgh merchants from Danzig was forced to land passengers and crew on the island after plague was discovered on board; at least 40 of the travellers died.

The Dry Boak in Scottish History

Did you know that, on his way to death and glory at Trafalgar, Nelson was seasick? *Mal de mer* has also been a strangely common phenomenon in the shaping of Scotland. Margaret, Maid of Norway, granddaughter of James III and acknowledged heir to the throne of Scotland, died in Orkney en route to her new home; the poor wee soul was only seven and succumbed to seasickness after a horrendous passage across the North Sea.

An element in the Scottish victory over the Norsemen at Largs in 1263 is said to have been the fact that the Norwegian fleet had been severely battered by storms for days prior to the Ayrshire tussle and most of the tough Vikings were literally under the weather.

The beautiful *Hebridean Overture* or *Fingal's Cave* is a remarkable composition when you consider that, on his 1829 visit to Staffa to see the famous sea-cave, the German composer Felix Mendelssohn was violently seasick.

In the nineteenth century, seasickness also formed part of the family lore of hundreds of thousands of Scots emigrants heading for a new life in North America or Australasia. These folk, crammed into emigration ships, were even denied that basic necessity when you're feeling miserable as death – privacy.

Next Please for the Yellow Bunnet

In days of yore, you had to take your entertainment where you found it. Cockfighting drew the crowds, executions – particularly involving dismemberment – were fun and public ridicule always figured high on the list. Edinburgh magistrates were ordered by the Privy Council, the nation's legislative body, to erect a stone pillar near the Mercat Cross in 1606 where bankrupts were to be placed wearing the traditional yellow bunnet. As if it wasn't bad enough that you got your sums wrong! Crowds flocked to pour scorn on these crestfallen business folk, who were usually expected to undergo an hour of this very public humiliation.

Fangs, Dripping Blood

Spooky Slains Castle, clinging to the Aberdeenshire clifftop near Cruden Bay, is said to have been the inspiration for Bram Stoker's *Dracula*. The writer stayed at the Kilmarnock Arms Hotel in the town. The vampire legend was first depicted on the British stage in a production in 1820 with *The Bride of the Isles*, set on the Hebridean island of Staffa.

Queen of the Wash-House

A few days before her successful escape from Loch Leven Castle in 1568, Mary Queen of Scots tried to flee her island prison dressed as a laundress. Some eagle-eyed boatmen who noticed her delicate lily-white hands unmasked her. 'Never did a day's work in her puff wi' hauns like yon,' the vulgar boatmen no doubt told the waiting reporters as she was cairted off.

Mission Impossible?

Dr Archie Cameron, brother of 'Gentle Lochiel' of the '45 uprising, was hanged at Tyburn in London in June 1753 – the last man in Britain to be executed for being a Jacobite. He had returned from France, it was rumoured, to recover Bonnie Prince Charlie's gold, which was thought to have been buried in the vicinity of Loch Arkaig.

The Auld Tricks Are Best

Amazing, isn't it, how tried and true techniques seem to last the course. In the sixteenth century, nauseous Glaswegians relied on the technique of mixing wine with radish as a means of encouraging vomiting. If all else failed they were advised, 'Put your middle finger in your mouth as far as you can reach and this will help.' We know, we know.

No Rest for the Wicked

The habit of keeping long-murdered but unavenged Scots nobles above ground until they became a public health hazard was deplored in the 1590s by Scotland's Privy Council, which demanded that the Earl of Moray and Lord Maxwell, who had been lying around for months, should be interred within 20 days.

On the same unsavoury theme, one of the Stuart kings' strange preoccupations was bringing to trial subjects who had defied the Crown, even though they had shuffled off their mortal coils years before. Logan of Restalrig suffered in this way because of his failure to render to the king a treasure said to be buried at Fast Castle on the Berwickshire coast. And so anxious was the Crown to bring the House of Huntly to heel, following their rebellious behaviour in the north, that the embalmed body of the Fourth Earl was cairted to Edinburgh for sentence – seven months after his death at the Battle of Corrichie in 1562.

Marvellous City of the Dead

Stirling's Old Town Cemetery – in use since 1579 – is a gem for the growing legion of graveyard fanatics. Among its occupants are: John MacFarlane, great-uncle to Butch Cassidy; Matthew Murphy, who was the last known survivor of the Thin Red Line in the Crimean War when he died in 1913; and stonemason John Service, whose ornate stone was used for target practice by members of the Jacobite army during the '45 uprising. The stone still bears the musket-ball marks.

Shaken and Stirred

There are several stories in Scottish lore about folk, pronounced dead, sitting up in their coffins during the funeral. Cataleptic sleep, a trance-like state, could so resemble death that, in centuries past, it may have resulted in premature burials. The story is told in the south-west of Scotland about the coffin containing the domineering wife of 'a sorrowing husband' being taken to the churchyard when it accidentally struck a dyke on a sharp corner. To the astonishment of the funeral party, the jolt roused the 'deceased' from her trance. According to the story, this intimidating woman went on to live many more years but when she died (for real this time) and the cortège passed the same spot, the husband whispered anxiously to the bearers of the coffin, 'Tak' tent o' the corner this time!'

Never Looked Back

The most famous bona fide case of a recovery after execution in the Scottish annals is that of 'half-hingit' Maggie Dickson, executed in Edinburgh's Grassmarket but brought back to life by the jolting of the cart which was carrying her along the rough tracks to Inveresk churchyard at Musselburgh for burial. It's said she later married and had several children. If success can be gauged in these matters, Maggie now has a pub named after her in the Grassmarket. Immortality indeed.

There Won't Be Many Coming Home

Clan Farquharson could always tell their casualty total after clan battles using the Cairn of Remembrance near Balmoral. Each clansman laid a stone on the pile en route to the square 'Go' and then removed it on their return.

Love 'em or Loath 'em

The sad loss was reported, in combat on the fields of Flanders in September 1916, of a famous set of bagpipes belonging to a Major Anderson. The pipes had been played on polar expeditions in the early 1900s.

Incidentally, the popularity of pipe bands in Holland, the lilt of the Low Countries, is often linked historically to the early 1600s when Highland mercenaries fought in religious wars on the continent; many married local girls and settled in what is now the Netherlands. Non-Scots in Canada were apparently less than enthusiastic about the skirl of the pipes. One nineteenth-century Vancouver newspaper is said to have announced details of pipe band marches 'in order that ordinary citizens who are not Scotch can take to the woods'.

CHAPTER 7
Myth, Magic and Auld Mysteries
Odd Tales from the Tartan Edge of Reality

Amabo, Amabas, Amabampot

Alleged demonic possession could take many baffling forms. A strange case, which occupied the attention of the authorities in Duns in the Borders in the 1600s, concerned an illiterate, ignorant woman called Margaret Lumsden who was reported to be debating with officials in word-perfect Latin.

Beware the Third Day of the Ninth Month

Oliver Cromwell was, in so many ways, the scourge of the Scots but, remarkably, at least for students of coincidence, he recorded his two major victories over the Covenanters – at Dunbar (1650) and Worcester (1651) – on the same day: 3 September. Just to confirm the importance of the third day of the ninth month in the Lord Protector's life, he died on that date in 1658.

A Life of its Own

The impressive raven on the war banners and longship sails of the Norse Earls of Orkney was said to have a mys-tical life of its own: it could be seen to lift its wings in victory and allow them to droop in defeat. Some theorists suggest that the common association of the raven as a symbol of death in Scotland relates to the connection with the raven banner rather than merely his jet-black coat and his enthusiam for funerals.

Ventilation Guaranteed

Mary Queen of Scots' favourite, David Riccio – the Piedmontese lute plucker of Holyrood – was warned by an astrologer about his impending murder. You can excuse Davie for ignoring his advice. The astrologer, Damiot by name, had warned him to beware of 'The Bastard'. As Antonia Fraser has pointed out, in 1566 half the Scottish nobility qualified on that count, either by birth or behaviour. Eerily, however, it was the illegitimate George Douglas who is said to have delivered the first of 50 or so knife thrusts which ventilated and despatched the musician, who was also considered by the Reformers to have been a Papal spy.

Omens, Omens Everywhere

In 1639 a landslip exposed thousands of perfectly spherical stones from musketball-size to cannonball-size near Duns Law in Berwickshire. This was seen by the Covenanting army encamped nearby as a token of God's support for their cause.

Lucid in the Sky

Scotland seems to be a location where 'moonbows', arcs of the purest white light, are occasionally seen. For instance, people all over central Scotland noted this rare phenomenon at about 9 p.m. on St Andrews Day, 1623. As you might expect, they all guessed it was an omen of some sort, a portent of things to come – the only problem being that, on this occasion, no one seemed prepared to hazard a guess as to what it might signify.

She's No' in Yer Textbooks, Willie!

Caithness schoolmaster William Munro, a deeply rational sort of bloke, had dismissed stories about the existence of mermaids along the north coast of Scotland. Near Reay on the Caithness–Sutherland border he was, not surprisingly, stunned when, in 1809, in a deserted bay, he watched an 'unclothed female' sitting, combing her long, light-brown hair, on a dangerous offshore reef. A genuine mermaid sighting or a local lass, with a fabulous breaststroke, skinny-dipping – who knows?

Scotland's Shame

Dornoch in Sutherland was the scene of Scotland's last recorded witch-burning in June 1727, when Janet Horne was convicted of helping the devil to fit horseshoes on her lame daughter. The woman was burned in a tar barrel. Incredibly, that same year but in another universe, a group of London gentlemen first got together with a view to formalising the rules of cricket.

Famine Relief on Tap

In the hungry years of the 1600s, Scots often adopted the technique of the Masai tribe in Africa and mixed blood with their oatmeal, tapping a vein in the neck of a living animal when food was in short supply. Court records in the Highlands show prosecutions for 'vampirising' the laird's kye.

Oh, Precious Sleep!

A favourite torture of Scottish witch-finders in the sixteenth and seventeenth centuries was 'The Waking' – deprivation from sleep. Seemingly the most innocuous of all tortures, it achieved spectacular results. After a few days of being prodded and poked, shaken and shouted at, maddened by the misery of sleeplessness, the victims were ready to confess almost anything. Catholic martyr John Ogilvie suffered in this way during eight days of torture before his execution. Sleep deprivation caused 'perturbation to his brayne and compelled him ad delirum'.

Fly as Get-out

Perhaps Scotland's most unusual oracle in more superstitious times, when everything from the size of hailstones to the colour of a baby's hair was seen as portentous, was the immortal fly of St Michael's Well in Banffshire. Every movement of this much-revered fly was regarded with what was described as 'silent awe' and, if it appeared spirited or dejected, a prediction was drawn accordingly. A dejected fly? Obviously in need of a flychologist.

Bob's Awa' wi' the Fairies

Sixteenth-century Aberfoyle minister Robert Kirk translated the Scottish metrical psalms into Gaelic but is better remembered for his remarkable claim that he regularly visited the fairy folk beneath Doon Hill near the village. He even wrote a book, *The Secret Commonwealth of Elves, Fauns and Fairies,* based on his subterranean wanderings.

The Midas Touch

So fascinated by alchemy was King James IV that he had his own laboratory, complete with furnace, set up inside Stirling Castle. Here he often worked around the clock in the quest for the elusive formula which would transmute base metals into gold. Let's face it – even the monarch needs a wee hobby.

Feeding the Five Thousand – Melrose-style

During the reign of David I (1124–53), a 'grevious famine' prevailed in Scotland and almost 5000 starving countryfolk camped at the gates of Melrose Abbey. In a veritable 'loaves and fishes' event, Waltheof, the superior of the abbey, ordered them fed from the granary that had seemed almost empty of corn. This continued for a period of three months. A cynical commentator dismissed the strange events suggesting that the Church was not slow to promote a wee 'miracle', adding enigmatically that anyone who has seen a room with two doors will know the solution to the puzzle. Overnight re-stocking? It certainly looks that way.

Rose Among the Thorns

Perhaps the greatest enigma of Scotland's links with France concerns the building of the Earl's Palace in Orkney's windswept capital, Kirkwall. Considered by many to be the most accomplished piece of Renaissance architecture in Scotland, it was constructed during the regime of the Stewart Earls of Orkney – a rough-and-ready, illiterate crew who turned the islands into a forced labour camp. The identity of the cultured individual who prompted the building of this fairytale palace may never be known.

Our Glorious Eggs

Forget woolly mammoths encased in the tundra ice or the mummified remains of the rulers of ancient Egypt, Scotland has its own wee miracle of that ilk. In 1976 archaeologists working at Perth on the site of the Old Parliament Hall found two unbroken duck eggs which experts estimated must have been 600 years old. A missed breakfast for some overworked fourteenth-century MSP, perhaps?

Exposing the Earl o' Hell

Tradition has it that the distinctive round church at Bowmore on Islay was built in that unusual style to ensure that Auld Nick would have no shadowy corners in which to conceal himself.

Floating a New Act

Edinburgh-born Victorian spiritualist Daniel Dunglass Home made his name with his remarkable ability to levitate. In the era of floating trumpets and cascades of ectoplasm, Home was unique. In more than 1,500 recorded séances, not a single case of fraudulent activity was proved against him.

Home was resident spiritualist at a number of royal courts in Europe, including Paris and St Petersburg, and was banished from Rome in 1864 as a sorcerer. His remarkable talent for levitation sometimes manifested itself unannounced. At one dinner party he floated off a cushion and his attention had to be drawn to this by his host. The most famous lift-off took place in London when, in front of a crowd of witnesses, he floated out of a third-floor drawing room window and returned by an adjacent window which had been conveniently left open.

So Bad – it Must Be Good

Folklorist Ernest Marwick recalled in his survey of Orkney folk medicine that, even in the 1920s, one island doctor kept a barrel of foul-smelling green liquid in the corner of his surgery from which the ladies of the district filled their medicine bottles. At worst, it is thought to have been a mild laxative but it was so foul that, in the patients' view, it simply had to be effective.

Product of a Bad Pint?

In 1624 four Stirling gentlemen reported a strange phenomenon a few miles from the town – a phantom battle in the skies with the beating of drums and firing of cannon.

Such reports were common in the seventeenth and eighteenth centuries; there are even records in the south-west of folk witnessing visions of full-scale land and sea battles up-a-ky (in the sky). My own favourite tale is of the phantom army of Mid Stocket Road. In 1719 in Aberdeen, a silent army several thousand strong, apparently in the throes of a battle, was seen by dozens of people. A few months later, this spectral host reappeared and this time was seen by hundreds of people who had been attending the market in Old Aberdeen. Many were reported to have walked unaware through the ghostly ranks before being urged to look back by other witnesses. The experts have offered all sorts of explanations for these events, from meteorological conditions to religious frenzy. As far as I know, however, no study has been made to discover what proportion of these odd experiences followed a night in the pub.

A Word in Your Shell-Like, Jamie

When James VI attended the trials of the North Berwick witches in 1590, one of the accused was able to tell the astonished king all about the sweet nothings he had whispered in his bride's ear on his wedding night. These revelations are said to have convinced James of the reality of the Black Arts. He even wrote a book on the subject.

The first mention of Macbeth and the three witches, which Shakespeare so successfully plagiarised, comes in Andrew de Wyntoun's *Chronicle of Scotland.* Wyntoun (1355–1422) was prior of St Serf's on Lochleven. There are also unsubstantiated rumours that it was James VI who encouraged Shakespeare to include the trio of hags in his *Macbeth.* However, there may be an even more intriguing explanation for the presence of the witches in the play. Lawrence Fletcher, 'the chief of Shakespeare's company' is recorded as having visited Aberdeen in October 1601 with a party of comedians. It has been suggested that the bard himself was in the party. There are indeed a number of striking similarities between the fictional activities of the witches in *Macbeth* and 21 poor women, mainly sad old spinsters whose only crime was loneliness, who were burned in Aberdeen as witches in 1596/7 for a variety of offences, including raising an ill-wind. We'll probably never know the truth of it.

Ramming Home the Point

Astrology buffs might be interested to know that Aries (21 March – 20 April) is the sign which crops up most frequently in scanning the significant diary dates in Scottish history. Among the most important events under the sign of the Ram are the coronations of Robert Bruce, Malcolm II and James II. Also James VI, King of Scots, inherited the English throne; the Darien adventure finally collapsed; and, not least, the Wembley Wizards thrashed England 5–1.

Too Much Information

The fishing villages of north-east Scotland were always hotbeds of superstition. There is a multitude of words which were never, ever to be used at sea and a long list of people to be avoided as the fishermen made their way to the shore. These included ministers, skelly-eyed individuals and women with flame-red hair. The cross-eyed, red-haired female minister would have been a genuine cause for concern!

We must also remember that superstition was not restricted to the seafarers in that part of the world. In Buchan it was believed that, if the reapers arrived at the cornfield having planned the cut well in advance, they would find the heads of the corn empty. However, if they arrived not having said anything beforehand, the heads would always be full. Now you know how we came by the phrase 'ears of corn'.

Beyond the Veil

St Oran, a follower of Columba, is one of Scotland's forgotten saints – and possibly with good reason. According to legend, he agreed to be buried alive to appease a demon which was hindering building work on Iona. Sensationally, when the body was dug up three days later, Oran sat up and announced the rather upsetting news that there was no God and no life beyond the grave. Columba, we're told, ordered the earth shovelled in again on this unwelcome messenger.

Surprise, surprise

Professor Archie Roy of the University of Glasgow, astronomer and Scotland's leading investigator of parapsychological phenomena (a ghost-buster to you and me), once famously remarked, in a debate about life after death, 'If I find on dying that I no longer exist, then I shall be very surprised.'

You Can Lead a Horse to Water

Belief in and fear of the fabled waterhorse, the kelpie, of the Western Highlands was so strong in Skye, even as late as the 1870s, that a netting operation was attempted at Loch Nan Dubhrachan. During the search for the beastie, the net snagged on a large, submerged object. That was enough for the nervous kelpie-busters, who fled for the hills believing they had clearly proved the creature's existence.

Mystic Ahead of the Game

Perhaps the greatest Scots sorcerer – barring Ally McLeod who made us believe the world was our footballing oyster – was Borderer Michael Scott. A medieval monk who studied at Oxford and Paris, he lives on in popular legend as a wizard of repute. He wrote an 'all-powerful' book, most of which has now been lost. But it is said to have discussed, years before the Battle of Bannockburn, subjects as esoteric and contemporary as parallel universes and time travel. He gained an impressive reputation throughout thirteenth-century Europe and is reported to have charted the manner of his own death. Scott foresaw that he would be fatally injured by a small stone of a specified weight which would fall from the sky. Apparently he had a special helmet made in anticipation of this upcoming bump on the napper but, during a church service – when the helmet was removed – a piece of masonry did indeed fall from the vault slightly wounding him. He weighed the stone, found it to be exactly as he predicted, put his affairs in order and waited for death, convinced that, no matter how long this took, the stone would be to blame and the prophecy fulfilled.

Down in the Depths

Legends of loch monsters which mirror that of our own Nessie are found all over the world. My own favourite is Nessie's cousin in Okanagan Lake in western Canada, who is known by the splendid name of Ogopogo.

Legend of the Bleeding Tree

One of the most gruesome legends from Scotland's gory past concerns the bleeding ash tree of Cowal. The Campbells, having secured the surrender of a group of Lamonts in 1646, broke the truce and callously hanged and knifed dozens of clansfolk. The tree where they were strung up in Dunoon is then said to have died and, when cut down, a spring of blood issued therefrom. Quite naturally, it became a tourist attraction before being dug up by the Campbells in an effort to destroy the legend. They failed – probably because, as the secret mythic equation ($l = r + t$) reveals, a legend is simply a rumour with time added.

The Cosmic Joker at Work?

The discovery of amphibians apparently sealed within rock which, on being released, appear to be restored to life have been reported all over the world and there are several instances in Scotland. A frog cut out of a block of coal at a Kilmarnock pit lived for a short time and, in 1821, at Auchtertool near Kirkcaldy, a mason dressing a millstone cut away the stone to find a lizard embedded inside. After being exposed to the air, it lived for half an hour. This is a convincing episode because reports indicated that there was an accurate impression of the lizard in the stone. There was no fissure of any sort in the rock, which had been 22 feet below ground level. Cynics suggest that the creatures were contemporary and had simply appeared at an opportune moment from offstage, but others point to the fact that frogs hibernate in the hard mud beds of pools and streams before popping out in warmer weather, none the worse for their entomb-ment. The difference between a few months' snooze and countless millennia sealed in stone still gives pause for thought.

Travel Expenses Included?

The job specification for witches and warlocks in early modern Scotland was a very wide one and didn't always involve the mixing of potions involving frogs' legs and cat urine or the casting of spells to make your neighbour's testicles shrivel. In September 1583, Kate the Witch was secretly hired by the Earl of Arran for 'a new plaid and six pounds' to harangue Walsingham, the English ambassador, wherever and whenever he appeared in Scotland.

Too Much Toil and Trouble

An eight-week course in witchcraft scheduled for the high school in Bellshill, Lanarkshire, had to be cancelled in the 1980s following an angry reaction from the local member of parliament. The education authority said, however, that the main reason for cancellation was a lack of interest. The practical folk of Bellshill felt that wizardry came a poor second to cordon bleu cookery and basic car maintenance. Mind you, that was in the pre-Harry Potter days.

The Ghostly Roll

Drake's Drum, named after the English naval hero, is a ghostly beat which has been heard by the British Fleet on a handful of occasions at moments of great national significance. One of the more recent occasions was at the end of the Great War when the surrendering German Imperial Fleet arrived off the Firth of Forth to be met by the British battle fleet. Through the hours of tense naval manoeuvring, the single drum rang out from deep in one of the battleships. A thorough search was made but the phantom drummer was never found. All the ship's band were at their firefighting positions and – even more eerily – all the band's instruments had been locked away. This legend stemmed from Drake's promise to the people of England, on his deathbed in the West Indies, that he would come to his country's aid in times of national crisis. The drum itself still hangs in the family home in the West Country.

Adopt a Witch

A bizarre website was established at the beginning of the twenty-first century to ensure that the memory of every so-called Scottish witch is preserved. It immediately caught the public imagination. The pagan group who set up the site hope that people will adopt a witch to prevent them becoming lonely in the afterlife. Some of the more famous Scottish witches such as Janet Douglas, burned in Edinburgh in 1557, were quickly snapped up.

CHAPTER 8

Oddities, Absurdities and Cauliflower Ears

Scotland's Many Strange Faces

Splendidly Shoogled!

Seasoned tram drivers in Glasgow were easily identified apparently – by their crumpled cauliflower right ears. The deformity was caused by the open design of the old cabs, which were completely exposed to the weather. Cartilage erosion of the exposed ear often resulted.

Day of the Bent Penny

1 September is the day in Glasgow to get yer bent penny oot and have a good greet. On this day in 1962, the last official Glasgow tram journey was made on the legendary run from Dalmuir West to Auchenshuggle. Thousands of people turned out and many laid pennies on the tracks for the caurs to make their lasting impression. Auchenshuggle, by far the most romantic terminus name on the old network, was located in the city's London Road. This famous spot took its poetic name from the fields of swaying corn which surrounded the site when the service began to operate.

Some of these wonderful machines can still be seen at Glasgow's Museum of Transport. In Aberdeen, as always, they did things differently. The last trams were ceremoniously, if a bit thoughtlessly, incinerated at a public bonfire in 1958.

Tram World

The junction of Renfield Street and Jamaica Street in Glasgow's city centre is said to have been the busiest in the world, with 516 tram cars negotiating the crossroads every hour on a Saturday night. In 1948 the system carried an incredible 516,673,261 passengers.

Andy's Heart Was in the Right Place

The little cable cars which climb halfway to the stars in San Francisco were the brainwave of immigrant Scot Andrew Smith Hallidie. Although these were once found in many US cities, San Francisco has the last fleet of wee caurs. In 1900 the city had 110 miles of line and 600 cars but by 1980 it had only ten miles and 40 cars.

Steaming Towards the Big Idea

A mini health revolution in Scotland began in 1848 when the Black Isle scholar and adventurer David Urquhart wrote about Turkish baths in a travel book. Hot-air baths followed by 'soaping, washing, rubbing and kneading' were soon popular.

Creative Lunchbreak

During his dinner break at the University of Glasgow in the High Street, Greenock's James Watt was accustomed to taking a stroll on Glasgow Green. During one of these dauners he is said to have hit on the idea for his reciprocating steam engine. Arguably the outcome of this piston stroke of genius was nothing less than the Industrial Revolution.

Baiting the Bard

If, in the modern style, you'd called our national bard 'Rabbie' to his face, he might well have smacked you one. In Ayrshire this usage was a name reserved for a dunderheid and the poet himself preferred Rob, Robin or Rab.

Gun-Totin' Sycophants

George IV, on his famous 'tartan' visit to Edinburgh in 1822, had to retire early from a crowded dance at the Assembly Rooms when an over-enthusiastic Scot dropped his pistols on the king's big toe in the rush to be officially presented to the monarch.

Accuracy Is All

Newspaper reports of the nineteenth century could be masterpieces of fine detail. In September 1856, a hungry Glasgow shipyard labourer was jailed for ten days for stealing two slices of bread (unbuttered) and four slices (buttered).

City of the Silver Darlin's

Glasgow can boast its own miracle of the fishes. A few hundred barrels of herring laid the foundation of its reputation as a great trading city. In 1688 a merchant called Walter Gibson, using a hired Dutch boat, sent the fish to France from where it returned with salt and brandy, which was sold at a smashing profit. Encouraged by this success, he bought the boat and began to trade with Europe and the American colonies. Glasgow the Merchant City was up and running.

Testing the Tossers

The ultimate Highland Games challenge – the Braemar Caber, almost 20 feet long and weighing in at 122 lb – was replaced in 1984 by a longer pole to make things a 'wee bittie more difficult' for the tossers, despite the fact that only a few of the heavies had managed to heave the old one correctly.

The Game's the Thing

The first properly organised Highland Games in the recognisable modern form was probably held by the St Fillan's Society in Perthshire in 1819. It's claimed that this event also saw the first-ever competitive sword dance. However, Highland dancing was a 'men only' event until the late 1800s when a brave lady from the Douglas family made the breakthrough and danced along too, dressed identically to her male counterparts.

Interestingly, the Highland Games appear to have a longer 'official' pedigree in the United States where, before the American War of Independence in the 1770s, Scots soldiers stationed in Georgia competed against Creek Indians in the first recorded North American Highland Games. Nowadays there are upwards of 125 Scottish Highland Games held annually in the States and many more in Canada, Australia and New Zealand.

Davie's Smart Move

Textile pioneer David Dale boosted his workforce at New Lanark by 100 when he learned in 1791 that a ship with 400 emigrants heading for North Carolina had been forced into Greenock by a storm. He calculated correctly that a significant number of the would-be settlers would already be scunnered at the thought of the Atlantic crossing. He offered contracts to the waverers and a quarter of the passengers took up the offer to work at the pioneering mills at New Lanark.

Naming the Outsiders

The word 'Sassenach' is these days universally used by Scots in a mocking manner when specifically describing their English cousins. But the expression actually means someone foreign to Scotland – English or otherwise – and was originally used by the Gaels to describe Scottish Lowlanders.

Silly Girls

In the 1950s, Glasgow's razor-gang, cut-throat image prompted film star Diana Dors to go slightly over the top when she commented, 'I'm terrified every time I think of Glasgow.' In the same vein, American actress Julia Roberts declared that she would rather starve than eat haggis. Nae wonder Miss Roberts is on the scrawny side – to such an extent that she has to walk about in the shower to get wet.

Grey Granite and Hard Hearts?

Marischal College in Aberdeen was opened in 1906 on the site of the educational establishment which first took in scholars in 1593 and is said to be the world's largest granite building after Seville Cathedral. The ungrateful, granite-hard heart of Aberdonians is one of Scotland's greatest myths, yet the stories persist. Perhaps the unkindest quote of all is attributed to a (not surprisingly) anonymous city minister who once prayed, 'Thank thee, O Lord, for all thy mercies, such as they are!'

Not Part of the Calculations

Eighteenth-century Scottish economist Adam Smith – who wrote *Wealth of Nations* and whose theories still have a profound effect on economic thinking the world over – was kidnapped by gipsies at the age of four. During the ensuing search, his captors abandoned him.

Smith, Kirkcaldy's most famous son, did not dwell overlong on trifling issues such as consistency of spelling in his masterwork. He used 'publick' and 'public' in his text, as well as 'complete' and 'compleat' and 'independent' and 'independant'. To be fair, dictionaries had just begun to make an appearance. The full title of his book, incidentally, is *An Inquiry into the Nature and Wealth of Nations.*

Adam Smith was chosen by American historian Anthony Hart as one of five Scots who made the top 50 list of individuals who had most influenced the lives of their fellow humans. The other Scots were James Watt, James Clerk Maxwell, Alexander Graham Bell and Alexander Fleming. These Superscots joined the likes of Christ and Mohammed in the big league. By contrast, the 2002 poll run by the BBC to find the Greatest Briton (Winston Churchill) had no Scots in its top ten. Alexander Fleming, the man who discovered penicillin just made the top 20, while Scotland's Mr TV, John Logie Baird, got the forty-fourth slot, just behind Radio 1 DJ John Peel! Ah, fickle fame.

Becoming Bookish

In the 1500s the Scottish public began to get the reading habit. Among the more popular of the early books were *The Seeing of Urines*, *The Overthrow of Gout* and *Interpreting Dreams.* Yet, even in 1735, Glasgow – despite its already famous university – was considered too small to support two booksellers. In fact, it didn't have a public library until 1791. The *Encyclopaedia Britannica*, which you now require a second mortgage to purchase, was first published in Edinburgh in 1768, in parts costing 6d each.

Fun by the Ton

In 1936 the ancient royal burgh of Peebles, 20 miles south of Edinburgh, decided to put itself on the tourist map. Already recognised as a spa centre, it went flat out to attract visitors with a campaign slogan which read, 'A Holiday is a Non-Stop Jolly Time in Peebles.' Another 'haud me back' situation?

Get up an' Gie Them a Blaw

One reason given for the Jacobite defeat at Falkirk in 1746 is that the regimental pipers, who should have sounded the clan rallies, had given their instruments to the camp followers and, instead, were getting stuck in with dirk and sword.

The Skirl o' the Pipes

Piper George Findlater of the Gordon Highlanders was badly injured at the Heights of Dargai on the North-west Frontier of India in 1897. He gained the Victoria Cross, having continued to play to inspire his colleagues despite being wounded in both ankles. And the tune he played is thought to have been the stirring 'Haughs o' Cromdale'. Mind you, the world is changing. In 1983 the Western Isles Council, unable to find a local bagpipe instructor to teach in the island schools, gave the job to a pipe-major from the Lowlands.

Have I Got Tepid News for You

In the late 1600s Thursday took on a very special significance in Edinburgh. It was the day when news of the previous weekend's English parliamentary business and goings-on at court in London came into the public hands in Scotland after being brought north by fast horse.

Nothing for Me?

Even into the 1700s, a mail delivery was such an event in Hawick that when letters arrived they were set out on a stall on market day to be claimed. This attracted great interest, particularly from those poor souls who never received any correspondence.

Thor at Work in Parkhead

Of all the clattering and banging which characterised the bustling industrial metropolis of Glasgow in the late 1800s, no sound was more
impressive than the Sampson Hammer at Beardmore's Parkhead Forge.
Buildings nearby began to crack as the great steam hammer dropped
on to the steel slabs being prepared for rolling.

Some Christmas Crackers

When James VI went to London in 1603 to assume the English throne
from Elizabeth, he took with him the old Scottish prejudice against pork
(said to suggest that the Scots were a lost tribe of Israel). James,
searching around for an alternative Christmas platter, 'discovered' the
turkey. Arab traders, commonly called Turks – had brought the bird
(originally from Mexico) to North Africa.

Oddly, in Turkey the bird is called the 'India', in Portugal it is known
as the 'Peru' and the Gaelic word for turkey translates as 'French
hen'. With a schizophrenic pedigree like that it is little wonder that
the Scots king and his subjects north of the Border became hooked
on that most gormless of birds, marvellously titled in auld Scots as
'bubbly jock'.

Seasons Greetings

The idea of Christmas cards is said to have originated with Leith
publisher and bookseller Charles Drummond who, in 1841, produced a
wee New Year card which read, 'A Gude New Year And Mony O' Them'.
London printers soon saw the possibilities and produced glitzy and
elaborate Victorian cards for the Christmas festival, which was always
more popular in the south.

Christmas in Scotland has really only been celebrated with any
degree of enthusiasm since the end of the Second World War. Indeed,
Christmas Day only became a public holiday in Scotland as recently as
1958 and into the 1960s there was still a postal delivery on the big day.
When Charles Dickens misread the inscription on a tombstone in
Edinburgh's Canongate kirkyard in 1869, the famous *Christmas Carol*
character 'Scrooge' was born. In the twilight, the novelist read

'Ebenezer Lennox Scroggie Mealman' as 'Meanman', and the hard-hearted legend was born. In fact, the original Kirkcaldy-born Scroggie, according to journalist Peter Clarke, was a warm-hearted, kindly individual – more like Scrooge redeemed, in fact.

Covering a Multitude of Sins

If you're looking for someone to manufacture a gargantuan umbrella, then where better to look than Rain Town itself – the great, dripping city of Glasgow. In 1888 city umbrella manufacturer Wilson Mathieson of Glassford Street had constructed the largest umbrella in the world – 21 feet in diameter. Ironically, this was to provide shelter for an African king to entertain 30 guests beneath the blazing tropical sun. Umbrellas were introduced to Glasgow by a Dr Jamieson in the 1780s. He had purchased the first specimen in Paris and caused a stir in his home city when he raised it for the first time.

No Cover-Up

The date 2 May 1858 goes down in the annals of Glasgow criminology as the day a notorious umbrella thief who had been plaguing the Royal Exchange in the city was finally arrested.

A Transparent Winner

The world's first X-ray department was up and running in March 1896 at Glasgow Royal Infirmary – the moving force being Dr John McIntyre. One of the most famous early X-rays was that of Sir Harry Lauder's hand, which he agreed could be X-rayed as part of his charitable activities. He later signed the image.

Mobile Mac – the Sound Man's Nightmare

Lossiemouth-born Ramsay MacDonald's shifting style of public speaking meant that Britain's first radio election broadcast, in October 1924, was considered a failure – with the mercurial Labour leader wandering away as usual during his speech, too far from the fixed microphone to make the experiment a success. The first radio transmission of an opera had taken place the previous year in Glasgow, with a microphone being placed frontstage at the Coliseum Theatre.

Don't Mess with the Money Men

The town of Carluke in Lanarkshire has an unusual claim to fame in that it was the home of J G Jarvie – the man who introduced the concept of hire purchase to Britain after seeing it in operation in the United States.

Simmer Gently

The first coins to be put into general use in Scotland were, in fact, made across the Border in Carlisle in 1136. Over the next few centuries, counterfeiting was frowned on to such an extent in medieval Scotland that in 1398 a false coiner was ordered to be boiled to death in Edinburgh.

Eagle who Soars Above the Glen

Although the wearing of tartan was banned in Scotland for almost 40 years after Culloden, a quiet export trade took tartan to the Native Americans, who were said to be completely sold on the bright colours. It has been argued that the Scottish Highlanders assimilated best with these peoples because of the similarities between their tribal and clan structures.

Despite the post-Culloden ban, there was still a legal way in which the Highlander could wear the kilt and bear arms – and that was to join the British army. Thousands of Scots did just that and it is calculated that, between 1715 and 1815, 85 regiments were raised in the Highlands, the troops often being asked to lead the line. One of the main pressure groups, which eventually won a repeal of the ban, was the Highland Society of London, who argued for a repeal – not on the basis of national pride and martial dignity – but on the grounds that Highland dress would add substantially to social events.

It's said by those with nifty fingers that the Ogilvie tartan is the most complicated of all to weave: a sett of less than 12 inches has 91 different widths of red, white, blue, yellow and green colouring. There are now well over 300 officially registered tartans, including that of the US Seventh Cavalry – a navy-blue ground colour with lines of white, yellow, green and lilac and a broad red band. The tartan was adopted in tribute to the Americans of Scots descent who served with General George Armstrong Custer at the Battle of the Little Big Horn.

Not Knowing your Borealis from your Elbow

The most regular inquiry made over the years to staff at the Aberdeen and Grampian tourist offices is a stunner: 'What time do they switch on the Northern Lights?'

Long, Long Ding-Dong

Lanark has one of the oldest still-functioning bells in Europe, housed in the belfry of St Nicholas's church in the High Street. The bell is dated 1110 and is known to have been recast at least four times.

The Dark Clouds of Industrialisation

Nineteenth-century crofters' wives in the Inner Hebrides were able to trace Glasgow's growth as a centre of industrial muscle – the Second City of Empire – by a most novel phenomenon. When the wind blew from the south-east, their washing on the line was often flecked with soot and grime carried from the city's tall factory chimneys. When the wind blew from the opposite direction, various eruptions of Mount Hecla in Iceland caused clothes on bleaching greens to be stained by volcanic dust. It was estimated that, at the height of Glasgow's industrial development, 64 tons of soot and dust descended daily on the city from industry and coal-burning. Little wonder that Glasgow had one of the worst records in Britain for pollution-related consumption.

Mary, Mary, Quite Contrary

Despite the historical revisionists who want us to examine less glamorous aspects of Scottish history (such as worker organisation and the fluctuating price of turnips in the early 1800s), Mary Queen of Scots continues to command a place as perhaps not only the most romantic figure in the history of Scotland but also a figure of European significance. In 1911, over 300 years after Mary's execution, Queen Maria Christina of Spain refused to allow a crucifix, worn by Mary at her execution, to be exhibited in Scotland because of its special sanctity. Mary must have been laden with crucifixes on that last walk because another cross, said to have been worn on the fateful day, is in the possession of the Marquis of Ailsa, head of the Clan Kennedy, and is said to have been handed by Mary to her maid, Jane Kennedy, moments before the axe fell.

Dream a Little Dream with Me

Do you dream a lot and talk in your sleep? As an old philosopher friend of mine was wont to suggest, it could be a good thing and it could be a bad thing. Well, here's a salutory anecdote which suggests that it's most decidedly the latter. Such was the paranoia within the Catholic Church, as the first waves of the Reformation broke over Scotland in the 1500s, that Richard Carmichael, a singer in the chapel royal at Stirling, was sentenced to be burned at the stake for mumbling in his sleep that the devil should take away greedy priests. He was reprieved at the last minute but I'll bet he regretted that late-night cheese sandwich to his dying day.

Unlike the great Robert Louis Stevenson. The plot of *Dr Jeykll and Mr Hyde* came to Bob during a dream, it's alleged. After a bountiful supper of bread and jam, he awoke next morning and immediately began work on the master-piece. More cynical commentators suggest he may have been 'inspired' by the plot of James Hogg's marvellously Gothic thriller *Confessions of a Justified Sinner.*
In the 1500s, medical advice for a good night's kip urged Scots to 'cover your head in a close-quartered bed' – mind you, the same experts thought that combing your hair in the evening was detrimental to health.

High Chair for Wee Jamie

When one-year-old James VI was crowned in 1567 by the Protestant nobility, to replace his Catholic mother Mary Queen of Scots, a special chair had to be constructed so that he did not have to be plonked – a wee lost soul – in the vast throne. The very chair, it is claimed, is housed in a museum in Ottawa, Canada.

The Strange Stone Horseman

In the spring of 1685, there was great excitement around Edinburgh's Parliament Square when the country's first equestrian statue – of Charles II and costing the vast sum of £1,000 – was erected. According to one newsman at the scene, the statue caused 'much amazement among the vulgar people who had never seen the like'. Now this is where I can let you into a wee secret of the sculptor's trade. If you see an equestrian statue in which the horse has both front legs in the air, it means the hero on board died in battle. If one hoof is raised, he died from injuries received in battle and, if the four hoofs are firmly planted on the plinth, then the celebrity died a natural death.

Davy Jones's Bunker

Scotland's strangest coalfield lies on the bed of Scapa Flow in Orkney where hundreds of tons of what local people call 'sea coal' was dumped from the bunkers of German warships when they were being raised for salvage, having been scuttled by their crews at the conclusion of the First World War. By contrast, when convoys gathered at Scapa Flow during the Second World War, the cargo ships had nothing to take out to New Zealand and so were filled with Orkney sand as ballast. This was ditched at Wellington on New Zealand's North Island and, to this day, the beach at the city's Oriental Bay is covered with Scapa sand.

The Sugary Tide

In the 1970s, it's claimed that fish caught in the Clyde Estuary were found to have sugar diabetes. It was a result of the sinking of the Greek freighter *Captayannis* off Craigendoran near Helensburgh and the subsequent dispersal of some 8,000 tons of sugar into the river.

Too Close to Home

The familiar, but now probably politically incorrect Glasgow saying, 'Do you think ah came up the Clyde in a banana boat?', meaning, 'Do you think ah'm a daftie?', has special poignancy when you consider that the shipbuilders Stephens of Linthouse built some of the most famous banana boats for the West Indian trade.

Unspeakable Affection

In medieval times when people lived in close proximity to their animals, bestiality is thought to have been relatively common. The last person to be executed for this type of crime – after a long-term relationship with a mare – was Banffshire farmer Alex Geddes, in 1751.

Another Age, Another Life

The now sleepy Fife fishing village of Crail was, in the Middle Ages, the venue for one of the biggest, regular international markets in Scotland. Coal, salt, hides, herring, wool and woven textiles were exported through the Crail entrepot while imports were mainly timber and luxury items such as wine and fine cloth.

Floor with a View

The English poet Sir John Betjeman used to sit on the floor of Glasgow taxis when he visited the city, in order to get a better perspective on the fine Victorian and Edwardian buildings.

CHAPTER 9

Rivet Chuckers and Kilted Bachles

Entertainment, Sport and Politics

Places Please for the Egg-and-Spoon Race

The American track-and-field meets, which have seen US athletes rise to world dominance, evolved directly from the Highland Games – the organisers deciding early on to omit the more rugged events such as the three-legged race and the sack race. New York Athletic Club started 'Handicap' Scottish Games in 1868.

Watch Where You're Sticking That Brush

If you regard persistent mobile phones and badly aimed umbrellas (good name for a rock band!) as simply inevitable hazards facing twentieth-century city-centre pedestrians, then harken to the story of the chimney sweep who was fined half-a-crown in 1845 for carrying his brushes and rods in a dangerous manner on the pavement in Glasgow's Saltmarket.

Who Moved the Goalposts?

The strange muscle-tearing game of Australian Rules football was exported to Scotland by Aussie expatriates in the late 1800s, and Glasgow had 20 teams. By the 1920s, this sport had vanished from the city.

The King and his Wee Notebook

When Charles 1 visited Scotland in 1633, he was already scarcely flavour of the day as a result of his authoritarian style of government. At a meeting of the Scots Parliament, much to the discomfort of the assembled company, he sat noting the names of those who didn't vote for his measures. Later, one of them, Lord Balmerino, was charged with treason.

The Disputed Anthem

A debate has raged for two centuries over the authorship of that most Scottish of songs, 'The Muckin' o' Geordie's Byre', which Andy Stewart famously interpreted as 'The Cleansing of George's Cowshed'. Candidates are an Alexander Rodger from Bridgeton and the eccentric pioneer balloonist, James Tytler.

Another Scottish anthem which deserves to be better known is the tune 'Hey Tutti Tatti', not our first Eurovision Song Contest entry but by tradition the melody which was played by the house band to the Scottish army as they lined up against the English at Bannockburn. It was to this air that Robert Burns composed his celebrated song of patriotism and war, 'Scots Wha Hae Wi' Wallace Bled' – now the universally accepted title of the tune.

A Chorus of 'Please Release Me'

While working as a coal miner at Hamilton in the days before he hit the big time as the personification of the bachly kneed, tartan-bedecked Highlander, Sir Harry Lauder is said to have entertained his workmates with a repertoire of music hall and traditional songs while they were trapped for several hours by a rock fall. It's probably a surprise to learn that Sir Harry was not the first to cater for the desire – particularly among expatriate Scots in the United States – for kailyard capers and couthy Highland ballads. In the words of historian Tom Devine, a music hall entertainer called W F Frame took Carnegie Hall 'by storm' in 1898 with his tartan togs and comic songs.

Rock-Solid Defence

One of the most quaintly named Scottish football teams – Inverness Clachnacuddin – takes its title from the town's charter stone, which was used as a symbol to denote rights of land ownership before written contracts came into general use in Scotland. The Stone of Scone, better known perhaps as the Stone of Destiny, is considered by some scholars to be Scotland's principal charter stone. Others think it was merely the stone lid of a cesspit. Interestingly, the stone is said to have 'groaned aloud with thunder' if sat upon by anyone but the rightful heir to the throne. Lends credence to the toilet seat argument, perhaps?

A Less Complicated World

In this age of the £50 million football transfer and vast soccer stadia resembling gladiatorial pleasure domes, it's instructive to look at the accounts of the football authorities a century or so ago. In 1886, the annual general meeting of the Scottish Football Association heard that the balance to hand was £474 – scarcely enough these days to buy you a season ticket at most of the bigger clubs. Perhaps, in the light of results on and off the field, we may be heading back to those simpler days.

Sad Notoriety

Experts consider that the world's first major sporting tragedy was the seldom- remembered 1902 Ibrox disaster. Twenty-five people were killed and more than 500 injured during a match between Scotland and England when a section of wooden terracing collapsed. This match was also the first international to feature fully professional players. The crowd was 80,000 – 10,000 over capacity.

Hardly Room to Swing a Club

If there was ever any doubt about Scotland's claim to be the cradle of golf, you need only look at the statistics. In the late 1990s, there were said to be approximately 450 golf courses in Scotland or, weirdly, one for every 11,111 people in the land. Mind you, during the Second World War, golfing acreage was reduced when golf courses were asked to give over 20 acres for new farmland to help with the war effort. Greens were exempt.

Stats to Remember

The highest golf course in the United Kingdom is said to be at Leadhills in Lanarkshire and golf's first recorded hole-in-one was struck in 1868 by Tom Morris at Prestwick's eighth hole during the Open Championship.

Time to Adjust

When golf bags were first introduced to Scotland in the 1880s, the older caddies did not take kindly to this innovation. These die-hards continued to carry the clubs loosely under one arm in the traditional style and slung the new-fangled bag (containing the sandwiches?) over the other shoulder.

Cocks o' the North

In 1701, cockfighting – the most popular sport in Scotland at that time – was banned from the streets of Edinburgh because it was bringing commercial traffic in the city to a halt because of the huge crowds spilling out on to the thoroughfares from the cockpits. It was said that, at the time, the Scots capital had the 'best cockers' in Europe.

Around the same period, boys were encouraged at Shrovetide to bring fighting cocks to school for a day of 'sport'. The slain became the schoolmaster's property and formed an important part of his salary.

Keeping the Peace

That remarkable sixteenth-century inventor of logarithms, John Napier of Merchiston, lived a retiring life. He demanded complete tranquillity for his studies and, when he found that cockerels in his yard were disturbing the peace, he soaked some grain in brandy and threw it out there. For a wee while perfect peace reigned at Merchiston.

An Impressive Performance

Let's not forget about the hens. Ayrshire's Symington hen became a local legend in June 1859 when newspapers carried details of the latest colossal egg she had laid. It was said to be 8 inches by 7 inches and had – if you can believe it – been delivered without discomfort. 27 August 1790 was also a historic day in henlore. Smith, the notorious hen thief, was whipped and banished from Edinburgh for life.

Follow, Follow, Follow, Follow . . .

Scots painter George Gibson, who emigrated to America in the 1930s, joined the scenic art department at MGM pictures and was responsible for the legendary yellow brick road in the award-winning Judy Garland film, *The Wizard of Oz.*

Standing in the Shadow of a Gubbing

The momentous 1885 victory by Arbroath over Aberdeen Bon Accord by 36–0 in the Scottish Cup is much-quoted in football quiz competitions. What is possibly less well known is that, on the same day and in the same competition, just along the Tay shore, Dundee Harp beat another team from the Granite City, Aberdeen Rovers, 35–0. Altogether a poorish footballing day for the Granite City. What interests me about these matches is what might have been. In those unsophisticated days, the rules insisted that the teams changed ends after each goal. Without these interruptions, we might have been talking about scores which would have matched or overtaken those achieved in recent years by the English cricket team.

Chick Young – from the Mould of Walter Scott

Sir Walter Scott is thought to have written the first sports report of the modern era – coverage of a Borders football match at the turn of the nineteenth century. In recent years the trend has been to use ex-players for commentators and scribes, with all the unexpected joys for the English language that this can bring. The legendary John Greig, the Rangers stalwart wing-half, once remarked, in his incarnation as a football pundit during a match involving Celtic that the then manager, Davie Hay, always had a spare couple of fresh legs up his sleeve. Now there's versatility.

First into the Maul

Two Kincardine schoolboys, Alexander and Francis Crombie, who studied at Durham in the mid 1800s before coming to Edinburgh Academy, are credited with the introduction of rugby football to Scotland. Mind you, you can't help thinking that the idea of picking up the ball and stuffing it up yer jumper must have occurred to some enterprising footballer long before that.

A Culture of Cinematography

Regular visits by touring theatre companies and music groups to the more far-flung parts of Scotland really only began in the last decades of the twentieth century. Locals were occasionally confused by this novelty although they were not strangers to the wider world of entertainment. The story is told of a theatre group who, after spending all day erecting their set at Macduff, were earnestly asked by the hall-keeper, 'Well, fit film are we gettin' the night?'

It's also said that, in Greater Bernera in the Outer Hebrides, the audience showed their appreciation of the visiting company's performance not by applause but by whether they stayed behind to help stack the chairs. I myself have witnessed a performance by a wind quintet from the Scottish Chamber Orchestra, on my adopted home of Papa Westray, Orkney, when the island's newest arrival was breast-fed in the front row to the soothing strains of Mozart. The players, it must be said, took it all in their stride. They did not, I'm pleased to say, milk the applause.

Ruling the Waves

It's not without a certain irony that we hear the strident, aggressive version of 'Rule Britannia' which is chanted by English football fans. Kelso poet James Thomson, who gave up the ministry to seek his fortune in London as a writer, composed the melody. Another eighteenth-century writer, David Mallet, also claimed credit for having penned the tune – but, don't despair, he also was a Scot.

High on the Battlements

The question most frequently asked of Glasgow's red-jacketed city guides is, 'Where's your castle?' Despite its many cultural, architectural and historical delights, the city doesn't have one. In historical terms, Glasgow is a 'new town', with its rapid expansion really only beginning after 1750 when its population was still only 37,500.

To Be or Not to Be

Blackness Castle on the south bank of the River Forth doubled as Elsinore in Franco Zeferelli's haunting film version of *Hamlet*.

Principles Are All Very Well

King James VI, a lifelong opponent of tobacco, once described smoking as 'loathsome to the eye, hateful to the nose and harmful to the brain and in the black stinking fume thereof nearest resembling the horrible stygian fume of the pit that is bottomless'. Nevertheless, even with such strong views, James was forced, on one occasion, to put his aversion to one side. While out hunting, a storm sent his party scurrying for shelter in a pigsty. The stench was so overpowering that one of the group was given the royal assent to light up in an attempt to mask the smell.

Each to their Own

DANGER: a politically incorrect anecdote approaching! Heavy smoker Agnes McLay died at her home in Kilmarnock in 1898. For half a century she used tobacco and was in the habit of having a smoke every morning after getting out of bed. She was 100.

King of the Weed

The Ayrshire village of Dalmellington has many claims to fame, not least the fact that it is the home ground of the Hewitson clan. One of the most unusual facts about this former mining community is that a son of the village, Andrew McKairter, after serving a long apprenticeship among the fagmeisters in Holland, was given permission in 1674 to set up as Leith's, possibly Scotland's, first tobacco spinner.

And Then the Spectators Wept

Although, culturally, Scotland lagged behind the rest of Europe for much of the medieval period, our tournaments were famous and many top foreign knights made their way to Edinburgh or Stirling to test their prowess. One chronicle – Scottish, 1 would guess – tells us that these superstars of the jousting circuit were 'oftymes overthrown' by the Scottish knights.

French knights who came to Scotland in those days stunned the Scots when they were observed using wine from their native land as an antiseptic to bathe injuries on the legs of their horses. Surely there is no vin *that* ordinaire? By the same token, when the Scottish nobility were short of a war (not a regular occurrence in the Middle Ages), they would travel to London and the continent where they competed in splendid tournaments with the best lancemen in Europe – the medieval equivalent of the professional footballers' summer bounce game on a Majorcan beach. In France, Scots knights occasionally took part in vast mock-battles – bloody training exercises – which resulted in many casualties and suitably impressed the ladies of court. This is possibly the origin of the famous old maxim: 'Once a king, always a king, but once a knight's enough!'

What's the Point of This?

One of the most prized sporting trophies of medieval Scotland was a lance with a golden tip which was offered at the regular jousts staged by King James IV in the shadow of Edinburgh Castle.

There Are Places 1 Remember . . .

The Beatles' amazing worldwide success was launched in May 1960 when a rock 'n' roll tour of Scotland began with a concert in Alloa's Victorian town hall. At the time, the boys called themselves The Silver Beetles and other venues on this historic circuit included Inverness, Keith and Peterhead.

All Over Now

Born in the Fife village of Pittenweem, the late Ian Stewart, a fisherman's son, got together in 1963 with Brian Jones to form the Rolling Stones. He was quickly out of the picture, however, and the Stones went on to become, arguably, the greatest rythym and blues band of the twentieth century.

Past Nursing Their Wrath

At the height of Scottish suffragette agitation in the early years of the twentieth century, Holyrood Palace was closed because of the threat of so-called 'terror attacks' by angry, franchise-seeking females. Attacks on post boxes were common and even Robert Burns's cottage at Alloway was targeted.

Early in their campaign, the ladies realised what a publicity gift golf was. In 1912, they evaded police at Balmoral golf course and replaced flags on the greens with 'purple banners of a political nature'. Two years later there was great alarm when suffragette Rhoda Fleming leapt on to the footboard of the king and queen's limo at Perth and tried to smash the windows. Police saved her from an angry crowd which, the newspapers reported, 'threatened her with a rough handling'.

The Struggle Goes On

It was a long struggle for women to achieve a more meaningful role in Scottish society, even after suffragette agitation and the granting of the vote. In the early years of the twentieth century, a qualification had been offered at St Andrews University which would surely have had the feminist lobby of today blowing a gasket. Although attracting interest from all over the world, the LLA (St Andrews) was not a degree but signified a Lady Literate in the Arts – the equivalent of a Higher Local Certificate. How much progress had been made by the middle of the twentieth century is indicated by the fact that, in 1944, the Chief Constable of Fife insisted that women police officers were quite unnecessary.

Those Fifteenth-Century Punks

In the early 1400s, regular fairs, market days, weddings and even funerals provided the opportunity for ordinary Scots lads and lassies to indulge in the most popular dance of the day among ordinary folk, 'The Salmon', which apparently consisted of 'active leaps like those of the fish from which it takes its name'. What a marvellous picture of our ancestors pogo-ing around the alehouse to a bagpipe-and-fiddle accompaniment.

A Riveting Performance

Glasgow's reputation in the entertainment industry as a difficult 'gig' goes back a long, long way. In 1805, a young man was fined heavily for lobbing stones on to the stage and the orchestra pit during a show at the Theatre Royal in Queen Street. The orchestra pit at the city's Panopticon Theatre in the Trongate was covered with wire mesh to prevent the musicians being bombarded with rotten tomatoes, turnips, cabbages or even rivets hurled by the discerning audience. It was here that Stan Laurel made his stage debut.

The Music Man

The story is told of a concert by the legendary Sidney Devine, the Scots Gene Autry, at Ayr when the audience got a bit over-enthusiastic and a bottle was thrown from the rear of the hall. It struck a wee bloke in the front rank of tables on the back of his head. Sidney sang on regardless. The injured man got to his feet, blood pumping from his head wound, and shouted to the back of the hall, 'Throw anither yin, for Christ's sake. I can still hear ' im!'

Whisper It!

Shakespeare's 'Scottish play', *Macbeth* – which should never be mentioned in a theatrical setting for fear of bringing down not only the curtain but the entire theatre – has always had a strange, fated history. The staging of two versions of the play in New York in 1849 caused a heated dispute over different interpretations of the lead role, ending in a riot in which 22 people lost their lives.

C'mon Mabel, Manipulate That Axe!

The fare at Glasgow's variety theatres in the early 1800s was nothing if not varied. On the bill one winter's evening at the Tivoli Theatre – later the Gaiety – appeared: Miss Lottie Lunn, comedienne, burlesque artist and dancer; Mlle Raffin with her troupe of performing monkeys; Mr Arthur Farren, the great female impersonator; and Miss Mabel de Vena, club swinger and axe manipulator. Eclectic or whit!

Never Mind the Quality

Theatre-goers in Scotland in the early 1500s required a stamina which would stagger a modern audience – not to mention a good packed lunch. Sir David Lindsey's *Ane Satyre of the Thrie Estaitis* – a 'short narrative' – lasted nine hours.

Critics Everywhere

Following the arrival of James VI in London in 1603 to take over the Crown of England after the death of Elizabeth I, the perceived failings of the king and particularly his squad of Scottish entourage, or hingers-on, soon became one of the most popular satirical targets for playwrights and theatre companies.

The Play's the Thing . . .

In the late 1500s, as the new Reformation was at its sternest, a company of comedians – much to the surprise of all and sundry – were given permission, by the minister and elders at Perth, to stage a play, provided there was 'no swearing, banning or scurrility' which might bring the Reformed faith into disrepute. Aye, right, but did you hear the one about the meenister and the six-foot choirgirl?

Jamie's House Band

Earlier in the sixteenth century, when James IV went on tour around the castles of his nobility, he made sure the evenings by the roaring log fires in the great halls went with a swing. According to the court records, he usually travelled around Scotland with 'five loud minstrels' in his train.

Every Journey Begins wi' a Wee Push

The first historic voyage of Henry Bell's *Comet* in 1812 was not without incident. The vessel grounded on a sandbank in the River Clyde, opposite Renfrew, and the passengers had to climb overboard and push her free.

Malcolm the Interpreter

When Margaret, the Hungarian queen of Malcolm Canmore, confronted the Celtic clergy in her campaign to reform the church in Scotland along Roman lines in the eleventh century, she was unable to speak a word of Gaelic and had to ask her husband, the king, to translate. However, even people speaking the same language can get their lines crossed. Remarkable advances in communications in the past century – enabling nation to talk to nation through telegraph, telephone, internet, e-mail and text messaging – are not without a price. The story is told of a church where a large stained-glass window had been fitted – much of the cash coming from a rich American with a love for that part of Stirlingshire where the church is situated. The minister sent a cable inviting the benefactor to perform the unveiling but was stunned by a curt refusal. This was a great mystery because the American had always indicated a willingness to be present. The puzzle wasn't solved until an opportunity came to compare the cable sent with the one which actually arrived Stateside. When transmitted, the cable included the words, 'Thanks largely to the generous succour from America' but, in the message received, 'succour' had become 'sucker'!

Oh, Thou Great Steamin' Water Beastie

One of the great missed opportunities of Scottish literature would appear to have been Robert Burns's trip in October 1788 on a pioneering twin-hulled, steam-powered paddle steamer which charged across Dalswinton Loch in Dumfries-shire at the breakneck speed of

5 m.p.h. The general opinion is that Burns, who was a friend of the steamship engineer William Symington, was among the passengers on that historic day but he appears not to have been sufficiently moved to record the voyage for posterity – one of the most significant of the early Industrial Revolution.

But wait. On the theme of missed Burnsian opportunities, we should remember that in the spring of 1786, as a result of an energetic sex life and resultant threats from angry faithers, Burns was well ahead with plans to emigrate to Jamaica. He changed his mind at the last moment thanks to a letter of praise from Thomas Blacklock, commending the Kilmarnock edition of his poems. Come to think on it, these two 'non-events' in the bard's life probably deprived us of epics such as 'Steamin' on Dalswinton Loch' or 'Ma Wee Bit Biler's Bustit' and Caribbean classics in the style of 'To an O'er Ripe and Fallen Banana', 'The Planter's Saturday Night' or 'Bonny Kingston Bay'.

CHAPTER 10
Spectacular Cludgies and Mingin' Middens

The Scot as a Social Creature

Little Hut on the Prairie

Scots inventors such as Alexander Graham Bell (telephone) and John Logie Baird (television) are legion but our imaginative brothers and sisters have also made many less trumpeted – dare we say obscure – contributions the world over. In 1884, emigrant James Candlish, following his trade as a blacksmith in the town of Rawlins in Wyoming, built the original sheepherder's 'home on wheels'. With its own built-in bed and stove, the wagon enabled the shepherd to spend the night far out on the range guarding his flock. However, it took years to convince the tough sheepmen to abandon their customary practice of sleeping under the stars. But Scotland also offered America and the world something much more sexy than a prairie hut. Orcadians Andrew Thomson and James Driver, who immigrated to San Francisco in the late 1800s, are credited with the invention of the clasp fastening which made boiler suit fasteners and – glory, hallelujah – stocking suspenders possible!

Loo with a View

Arguably the most spectacular toilet panorama in Scotland is located in the dungeon of Tantallon Castle in East Lothian, set on a crag overlooking the River Forth. The rock-carved aperture in the cramped stone privy is poised above a 100-foot drop down the face of the cliff to the rocks below. If you peer down the pan – now redundant except as a sanctuary for the occasional sore-pressed tourist – you can see the gulls confidently wheeling below, unthreatened by falling faeces – unlike their forebears.

Keen to Impress

At a famous dinner in 1543, the Earl of Moray entertained Contareno, the patriarch of Venice. Moray arranged for a set of crystal to be smashed, as if by accident, and immediately replaced – apparently to prove Scotland's prosperity.

In with Both Feet

The butcher or flesher's bill for Christmas meals at Holyrood, Edinburgh, in 1528, included £13 6s 8d for 1,000 ox feet and 1,340 sheep feet. Wholesale butchering of animals for meat in Scotland was unknown until fairly recent times. In earlier centuries, every part of the animal had to be earmarked for customers before the 'flesh-caddie' took a knife to the beast.

Toilet on the Roof of the World

A Scots firm, Associated Metals, was selected in the early 1990s to construct a toilet which was to be located on the slopes of the world's highest peak, Mount Everest. The company normally produced sinks and commodes for hospitals, oil rigs and ships but, when the Nepalese government decided on a toilet to protect the mountain's ecology, the Scots answered the call. The loo, complete with wooden seat for warmth, is anchored to the mountain with ice pegs.

From one extreme privy to another: we know that toilets for the common Scot were non-existent in the mid 1500s but it seems they were thin on the ground for the nobility also. There is mention made of a dysentery sufferer at a dance at Holyrood Palace being directed to the privacy of a casement window, which apparently served as the public toilet.

They Didn't Take No for an Answer

The lairds of Newtyle, north of Dundee, simply loved playing host to passing travellers. So keen were they on hospitality that they kept a cannon aimed at the road past their estate, which they unleashed upon passing travellers who seemed unwilling to come inside and be entertained.

Tooled up for Dinner

Cutlery was virtually unknown in sixteenth-century Scotland and merchants and burghers were expected to bring their own spoons and knives when they were invited out for dinner – forks were unknown.

Hunger, even famine, was too often a spectre at the Scottish feast at that time. In 1550, the number of courses at meals was limited by law because of food shortages – archbishops were to have no more than eight dishes while the poor burgesses had to make do with three.

Security Minded

In the 1800s, there was tremendous mobility among farm servants in East Lothian. Normally, for married men, a house came with the job and they often took their own locks with them when they flitted to a new house. One ploughman reported how his door was studded with keyholes made to suit the locks installed by previous occupants.

Whaur's Yer Noah Noo?

Scotland is noted for her long-lived citizens but, on the island of Jura, there is a tombstone noting a claim of almost biblical longevity. Gilmour MacGrain, who died in the reign of Charles I in the mid 1600s, is said to 'have kept 180 Christmases in his own house'. A slip of the chisel, a wee fib or a minor miracle – we'll probably never know.

Something in the Air

In the long-life stakes, Aberdeen has always figured high on the world scale. Four residents, whose average age was 128, were recorded by the famous Dr Webster in his world longevity top 20. Something in the air, perhaps? There are a few clues to the secret of a long life, however. In 1853, a Tomintoul woman died at the age of 104. She had put her longevity down to a lack of luxuries such as tea. In Edinburgh, it's also worth remembering William Eadie, bellman of the Canongate, who married for a second time in the early 1700s – at the age of 100 – and went on to live for another 20 years.

An Icy Version of Hell

The austerity of the Scottish Sabbath astonished the more liberal visitors from the Continent during the eighteenth and nineteenth centuries. One Frenchman was stunned when, on returning from church with his Scots host, he was cautioned by his companion, 'Not quite so fast or people will think we're talking a walk.' The French novelist Stendhal visited Edinburgh in the early 1800s and concluded, 'This day [Sunday], consecrated to the honour of heaven, is the nearest thing to hell I have ever seen on earth.'

Oversalting the Parritch

The 'Day of the Big Porridge' took place in the Highlands on the Thursday before Easter – Maundy Thursday. If the winter had failed to cast up sufficient seaweed on the shore (a vital fertiliser in centuries past), a large pot of porridge was prepared with butter and a quantity poured into the sea at the principal headlands. Apparently, this guaranteed that seaweed would turn up in quantity. Just to ensure success, it was suggested, by the seasoned campaigners in the community, that the ceremony should be performed only in stormy weather. Canny folk, those witch doctors.

Give it Time

The act of making fine porridge is shrouded in almost Masonic secrecy. It's said that a Highlander married an English lass only to discover that cooking wasn't one of her strong points. In particular, she totally failed to master the art of porridge-making. On one occasion she burned the porridge and, in the ensuing panic, salted it three times. Placing the bowl in front of her husband, she awaited the inevitable explosion of wrath but her man sipped the lumpy, salt-contaminated burnt offering, smiled and declared, 'Ach, Jean, I kent fine that given time you'd learn the way o' it!'

Victorian Fast Food

In 1846, *The Inverness Courier* reported how a flock of pigeons flew over the house of a Lochcarron gent, who raced outside with his trusty musket and managed to shoot one. It dropped down the chimney and plunged into a pot of soup simmering over the fire.

Basic Fare

The diet in the Scottish Highlands in centuries past has been described as potatoes and salt herring one day and salt herring and potatoes the next. In the *New Statistical Account* of 1845, a Morven boy, when asked what his meals consisted of, replied, 'Mashed potatoes.' Accompanied by what, he was asked. 'A spoon,' was the earnest response.

Living on the Midden

Medieval Perth, like its twenty-first-century counterpart, was subject to regular flooding and was generally boggy territory. Archaeologists believe there may have been an official civic policy of raising the town up on its own rubbish. In places this accumulated to the depth of three metres in a couple of centuries.

Cobblers on Every Street Corner

Most of the ancient burghs of Scotland still have a foothold in the past – but the attractive Black Isle community of Fortrose perhaps more than most. Many medieval towns specialised in a particular trade and Fortrose at one time could boast 32 shoemakers.

Getting our Act Together

When a Roman fleet sailed up the east coast of Scotland in 80 AD in a planned show of imperialist might, the expedition succeeded only in bringing together the squabbling Caledonian tribes in opposition, probably for the first and – some cynics might say – last time.

It has to be noted, however, that, on dry land, the Romans left us some damn good roads. The Empire network extended at its maximum to around 150,000 miles. The most stunning statistic about this road system is that, barring sea crossings, of course, it was possible to travel from Scotland to Ethiopia – perhaps 2,500 miles – without leaving the Roman roads.

One of the famous distance slabs, which were found along the line of the Antonine Wall in Dunbartonshire, was sent on loan for exhibition to the United States but was lost in the Great Fire of Chicago in 1871.

Some Things to Chew Over

Regular reports over the years have confirmed Scotland as 'Gumsieland'. Around 40 per cent of Scots are said to have false teeth and Scotland has been declared the most toothless part of the United Kingdom.

Swallowed by the Sea

Thurso in Caithness still remembers the day the sea gave up her teeth. A woman, crossing the Pentland Firth in May 1938, lost her falsers overboard. A few weeks later, on the island of Stroma, a set of teeth was found and kept as a grim curio – the finders imagining them to be the gnashers of some poor, drowned mariner. By chance, a neighbour of the Thurso woman was visiting the island and, knowing the story of her friend's loss, felt instinctively that this was more than a coincidence so took the teeth home with her. The ivories and their owner were reunited, and their provenance was confirmed when she got stuck into an experimental bacon butty.

An even greater mystery involving false teeth remains unsolved, however. After a particularly heated debate at Glasgow District Council in the 1990s, a set of false teeth was discovered on the councillors' benches. The teeth were never claimed.

Ache of Convenience?

In the early 1700s the Duke of Hamilton was considered as a possible future king of Scots by the anti-Unionist lobby. He let the side down badly, however, when he failed to turn up for a crucial debate because he claimed to be suffering from toothache.

The Archer's Complaint

Medieval Scots ate no sugar and as result had fewer cavities than their twenty-first-century counterparts. Mind you, men in those far-off days often suffered from gum abscesses as a result of the technique used by archers to load an arrow which involved holding the bowstring in their teeth. A flossing too far?

Making Tough Guys Weep

With one slim volume – *The Natural History of Human Teeth* – East Kilbride physiologist and surgeon John Hunter (1728–93) transformed dentistry from what has been described as 'crude butchery' to a well-defined skill which, nevertheless, still has the power to make grown men cry.

Tongue-Twisters Galore

Milngavie (Millguy) has long been a nightmare for soothmoother newsreaders but it is only one of a myriad of Scottish place names which are not pronounced as they appear. Others include: Athelstaneford (Ale-sten-ford); Alyth (Ale-ith); Auchencrow (Edincrow); Faray (Fara); Glamis (Glams); Holm (Ham); Islay (Eyela); Kilconquhar (Kinnochar); Lerwick (Lerrick); Moray (Murray); Ravenstruther (Renstrie); Sciennes (Sheens); Tillicoultry (Tillicootry) – and there are many, many more.

Biblical Reference?

Residents of the picturesque Border town of Galashiels, which has its Braw Lads Gathering on the first Saturday in July, are quaintly known as 'Galaleans'.

One to be Careful With . . .

The north-east district and family name of Buchan has been spelled in dozens of ways over the centuries, probably as varied a selection as any other Scottish proper name. The most common include: Bochin, Bouthouchan, Bougwan, Bowchane, Buthquhania, Buwan. My own favourite, with no disrespect to the Buchanites, stirs a deep-seated nostalgia for the patois of my home city of Glasgow – Boghan. The name has also been a challenge to radio and television newsreaders over the past 50 years, who cheerfully succeed, despite their best efforts, in making it sound like a powerful adjectival expletive, as in 'The *Buchan* roads are jam-packed today'. Try it yourself.

What's in a Name?

It's a strange fact that the famous *First Book of Discipline* (1560–1), which outlined the programme of the Reformed Church in Scotland, was compiled by seven Johns – Wyndam, two by the name of Douglas, Spottiswood, Willock, Row and, of course, Knox.

The Epitome of Tranquility

During the Radical Unrest of 1819–20, the Lord Advocate of Scotland, Henry Cockburn, remarked, at one point, that the east of Scotland remained peaceful: 'Edinburgh was quiet as the grave, or even as Peebles!'

Taxi!

The rough, pot-holed streets of Edinburgh meant that, as late as 1778, there were only nine hackney carriages in the city, whereas there were 188 public sedan chairs and 50 owned privately by well-off families. The first sedan chairs, six in all, were licensed for public hire in 1687, with the main stance being outside the Tron Kirk, and most of the chair-bearers being tartan-clad Highlanders. A year later an even more significant event is noted in the records: the High Street and Cowgate in the capital were laid with pavements – at a time when residents of most other British and European cities were plootering around ankle-deep in 'mud'.

Cleanse the Causeway

It was a poet with the splendid Welsh name of Hugh William Williams who, in the 1820s, first coined the phrase 'Athens of the North' to describe Scotland's capital, indisputably (hauns up anyone who wants to argue) the most beautiful capital city in the world. Just to keep our feet on the ground, we should remember that, in the late 1700s, Erasmus Darwin, grandfather of the great naturalist, said he was guided to his lodgings through the dark closes and wynds of the city by the phosphorescence from the rotting fish-heads which littered the causeway.

A Rose by Another Name

Interestingly, 'The Flo'ers of Edinburgh', a popular fiddle tune, recalls, not – as you might expect – the joys of the Royal Botanic Gardens but the popular nickname for the stench that emanated from the open sewers between the tenements in the days of 'Gardyloo!' – the warning shouted when sewage was hurled into the street. There was great excitement when new technology allowed closets to be built jutting out over the wynds. This improvement meant that waste would still fall directly on the heads of pedestrians but did not foul the walls.

Buckets of Blood

You would imagine, wouldn't you, that archaeologists, looking for evidence of bloodletting, would concentrate on Scotland's many battlefields. Not so. In the search for buckets of blood, the experts have been most successful at the medieval hospital of the Holy Trinity at Soutra in the Borders. A village once surrounded this institution but, by the late 1700s, only two or three 'wretched' cottages remained. Bloodletting was a popular cure-all in the Middle Ages.

On Top of the Pile

Isn't it down Barnsley way that they declare, 'Where there's muck there's brass!' Never a truer word. Auctions of heaps of dung, prized as field fertiliser, always pulled in the crowds and were regular events in the medieval burghs of Scotland. In the 1800s, Andrew Nicol of Kinross pursued a case at the Court of Session in Edinburgh over a disputed dunghill. Known at Parliament House as 'Muck Andrew', he carried a detailed plan of the heap with him wherever he went and, for 30 years, was always ready to outline the sorry affair to anyone daft enough to listen to him.

Streets Paved With . . .

When Stirling-born John McLaren was appointed superintendent of San Francisco parks in 1887, he secured one important concession. He wanted all the horse manure from the city streets (an impressive annual total of many tens of thousands of tons) to aid his project for converting the sand hills around the bay into the splendid parks we see today.

Just the Job

In the virtually treeless islands of Orkney and Shetland in centuries past, all sorts of unlikely items were called into service as fuel for the fire – clods of grass, worm-eaten driftwood, seaweed, tax demands and, most unusually, pats of sun-dried cow dung. It was much favoured for giving a bright flame. On some of the more remote Orkney islands, I've heard it said that there was even an individual, a 'sharnspinner', whose job – if you'll excuse the usage – was to turn the cowpats on the green to ensure thorough dehydration.

The Hungry Years

In 1634, Orkney and Caithness were said to be in the grip of a particularly severe famine in which – despite or perhaps because of eating dogs and large quantities of seaweed – many perished. Famine was all too familiar to the people of the Highlands and Islands during the 1700s and 1800s but, in 1783, disaster was averted when the government sent up tons of peasemeal that was surplus to army requirements following the end of the American War of Independence. According to historian Dr James Hunter, 1783 was always remembered thereafter as *bliadhna na peasrach* – 'the peasemeal year'.

CHAPTER 11

The Caledonian Antiziggy

Forever at the Crossroads

When Things Are Going Just Too Well

This chapter title is in danger of being too smart for its own good. The Caledonian Antisyzygy (you'll note that I've sprinkled a little of David Bowie's stardust in the heading just to make it more accessible) is a smart-arse phrase you'll hear mostly from the lips of academics and thinkers (not mutually exclusive) and from sore-pressed under-graduates who have overdosed on Red Bull. It is an almost impossible concept to define but, if I'm picking up the signals correctly, it is to do with the basic contradictions which seem to plague the Scots: blind optimism (Argentina, 1978) and unneccesary pessimism (we'll pay for this fine weather). If you're none the wiser, others much more learned than I am have described the antisyzygy as the Scottish antithesis of the real and the fantastic, the sudden jostling of contraries. The best example, I suppose, is the way locals describe their home ground on the south side of the Clyde as 'Sunny Govan'. As Michael Munro, author of *The Complete Patter,* explains – it is a 'blend of love of your own patch tempered with ironic realisation of its shortcomings'. You won't do much better than that. (Incidentally, the technophobes among you will be pleased to learn that 'antisyzygy' has just given my computer spellcheck a nervous breakdown: *not in dictionary, no alternative spelling* . . . fizz, bang, crash.)

Too Much of a Good Thing

Fear and trepidation about events in the natural world in years gone by do not seem to make sense to us today but they do perhaps reflect some inbuilt national pessimism. In 1666, the plentiful supply of fish, including herring, reported in the River Forth – a source of delight you would have thought – was seen by some churlish dafties as 'a very ominous sign'. Mind you, such a mindset may be one of the most accurate gauges of Scottishness.

Our Part in the Ethnic Mosaic

A renowned military strategist, asked for the composition of the perfect army, suggested 10,000 Englishmen after a hearty dinner, 10,000 Irishmen who had just swallowed their second bottle and 10,000 fasting Scotsmen. In the same vein, an Australian academic, asked to name the mix which would create the most successful group of immigrant settlers, plumped for mainland Chinese, overseas Jews of the nineteenth and twentieth centuries and the up-and-at-'em eighteenth-century Scots.

Black MacDonna

According to legend Scotland was named after the Egyptian princess Scota who brought with her into exile Jacob's Pillow, or as it is perhaps better known, the Stone of Destiny, which reached Scotland via Ireland (Larne to Stranraer on the afternoon sailing, presumably). Interestingly, in our increasingly multi-ethnic Caledonian society, this would mean that our founding mother was black or at least a dusky brown. The Scottish–Ulster connection is deep and wide and enduring. The scale of the seventeenth-century government-led Scottish 'plantation' of Ulster, at the root of many of the heartaches of the troubled isle in the past three centuries, is indicated by the fact that historians believe up to 100,000 Scottish Protestant settlers, mainly from West Central Scotland, may have been resident in the north of Ireland by the late 1600s. Many of these, of course, moved on to America in the 1700s as the Ulster–Scots Presbyterians who provided much of the bedrock of the American Revolution.

The Independent Streak

Clan pedigrees were always a matter of extreme pride among the glens and the story is told of two Highland chieftains boasting of the remarkable length of their ancestral lines. One of them declared that his ancestors had come out of the Ark with Noah. Unfazed, his companion replied scornfully: 'Oor ancestors ay had a boat o' their ain!'

Don't Let Appearances Fool You

Two of the most consistently popular and stereotypically Scottish male first names are Alexander (or Sandy) and David. Both, in fact, have East European origins and were probably introduced in the eleventh-century with the arrival of Margaret, later St Margaret, a Hungarian princess who married Malcolm Canmore.

England's Loose Change

The so-called Equivalent Money, or £398,085 10s to be exact, was intended to create equality of trade under the Treaty of Union and arrived in Edinburgh on 5 August, 1707 in twelve horse-drawn wagons guarded by dragoons. Just like the English to pay the debt in five-pence pieces!

A Dodgy Curry

In 1504, records show that the Scottish court was a gey dreary place. King James IV's jester – Curry by nickname – had been banished from court because he was a plague suspect. Philosopher David Hume suggested that the regular sentence of banishment for capital offences, rather than execution, arose in Scotland because offloading the dregs of Scottish society on our English cousins seemed like another nifty means by which we could express our chronic hostility to England – or, in the patois, 'get up their humph'. South of the Border, there was no Crown right to compel a subject to leave the country.

A Plague on our Houses

Over the centuries, Scots have blamed our English neighbours for almost every conceivable misfortune. Not surprising then that plague, or the Black Death, was popularly known in Scotland as 'The Foul Death of England' or 'The English Pestilence'. The effects of plague on day-to-day life in Scotland were immense. In the high summer of 1606, the disease was spreading through Scotland with startling speed, particularly in the towns. One report on the first day of August said that Perth and Stirling were almost deserted. You can just see the sagebrush blowing along the High Street, can't you?

Over-Reaction by Burns

Blind Harry's fifteenth-century *Life of Wallace* was one of the young Robert Burns's favourite books. He read and reread it and is said to have been particularly moved by the account of the patriot's bravery during his brutal execution in London in 1305. It was one act, said our bard, for which he could never forgive the English. Mind you Aberdeen University historian, Aly Macdonald, has noted that Blind Harry would not have recognised Wallace if he'd popped up in his cornflakes.

Finding a Scottish Link

That great Scots singer, the late Bill McCue, was a noted patriot and used to tell folk that there were only three kinds of people in the world: those who were born Scottish, those who wish they were Scottish and those who have no ambition at all. The more cynical Professor Ted Cowan, a historian at the University of Glasgow, believes he has identified a fourth category: those who are Scots and don't want to admit it!

Men in Kilts

'Jacobite' was the name chosen by the supporters of the Stuart King James VII to describe themselves after he was deposed in 1689. The nickname persisted through the lifetimes of his son James VIII (The Auld Pretender) and grandson Bonnie Prince Charlie. The title comes, from 'Jacobus', the Latin for James. Today it is often seen as a wee bit derogatory, describing some misty-eyed individual wrapped up in the tartan myth, blind to the realities of modern Scotland and ready at the drop of a targe to re-stage Culloden in the hope of an improved result. Folk who should know better still perceive the '45 as an English/ Scottish affair but the hard truth is that there was widespread support for King George and the Duke of Cumberland among Lowland Scots. Mind you, this gets complicated because Highlanders will tell you that Lowland support for the Hanoverians is no surprise since Lowlanders are not Scots at all. And sometimes we wonder why we are a confused nation?

Too Hot a Wash, Perhaps?

Over the years, there has been regular wrangling among patriots about the correct colour of blue for the Scottish Saltire, our beloved national flag (also useful for keeping the sleet off during footie humiliations within the Arctic circle). What shade precisely is azure? Well, the Scottish Parliament bods tell us it's Pantone 300 which, frankly, sounds to me like a shampoo. However, one or two flagophiles believe that Scotland's good old, familiar St Andrew's Cross may not always have been a white cross on a blue background. Controversialists argue that it might just as easily have been a blue cross on a white background that may even have had, God forefend, a pinkish tinge!

Good for the Complexion

When George IV came to Edinburgh in 1822, during his infamous Tartan Visit, Sir Walter Scott, who had organised entertainment for the monarch, went on board the royal yacht anchored in the Forth. He pleaded with the king to defer his landing – despite the waiting throng – until heavy rain eased. As King Geordie adjusted his notorious pink tights, the eminent writer is reported to have declared to the king, 'I can only say, in the name of my countrymen, I'm just ashamed of the weather!' Speak fur yersel', Wattie.

Willie Balhope – Daft Patriot

A detailed examination of the Scottish Wars of Independence in the late thirteenth and early fourteenth centuries will turn up more 'bravehearts' than William Wallace, the now legendary son of a Renfrewshire knight and immortalised by Mel MacGibson on the big screen. (*Go back to England and tell them the Scots will never be defeated.* God, it's enough to make your sporran wilt.) It has to be said, however, that some of the boys seem to have been less than witty. Borderer William Balhope had lived in England for years but, when Edward I and his army stormed into Scotland in 1296, Willie headed north to join the Scots. Although Edward had taken control by the time the adventurer arrived, Willie, undaunted, armed himself with two swords and set off on a one-man campaign into England that took him as far as Alnmouth in Northumberland. There, challenged to acknowledge Edward as his ruler, he declined and was promptly put to death. Futile, vainglorious, daft – but very, very Scottish.

An Educated Guess

In this number-crunching age when accurate statistics are used to justify or condemn almost everything from birth control to buying a bar of chocolate, it's hard to realise just how sparse hard facts were in centuries past. In 1706, when the crucial debate on the Union with England was under way, there was nothing remotely approaching a census available. Two high-profile activists, Fletcher of Saltoun and Seton of Pitmedden, disagreed on population figures: Saltoun thought Scotland's population was around 1,500,000, while Pitmedden put it as low as 800,000. These figures were crucial in terms of potential tax liability. Later calculations suggest that the real figure was just over one million.

Hanoverian Veto

St Giles Street was the name originally planned for Edinburgh's most famous thoroughfare – Princes Street. But, in 1766, when George III heard what was being suggested for the New Town, he blew his stack saying that it reminded English folk of the most disreputable parts of London. Royal pressure, of course, won the day and Scottish criticism was silenced.

The Long, Long, Long Memory of the Scots

We Scots never hold grudges, do we? Not much! Visiting an English county town, Sir Walter Scott is said to have called the local doctor to see to one of his servants, who had taken ill. The great man was astonished to discover that the physician was a former blacksmith and amateur vet from the Borders who had come south, settled among our English cousins and set himself up in business as a general practitioner. Scott, anxious about this clandestine change of occupation, asked, 'But John, do you never happen to kill any of your patients?' The 'doctor' explained that some died and some didn't and added, thoughtfully, 'Ony how, sir, it will be lang before it makes up for Flodden.'

It's also clear that, even away from the battlefield, there was, in medieval times, very little love lost between Scotland and England, the auld adversaries. For example, the eleventh parliament of James II declared that no Scotsman should marry an Englishwoman without royal approval, under pain of death.

Get into Line, Geordie

In 1714, a declaration was issued by James VIII from exile in Lorraine stating that, apart from himself, there were 57 descendants of James VI of Scotland and I of England with a better claim to the British throne than George I.

Out of Sight . . .

The wild, independently minded Scottish clans remained a sair trouble to the monarch even after James VI packed his bags in 1603 and headed for the bright lights of London. A saying which was often heard in seventeenth-century Scotland, and which well illustrates the autonomy and free spirit enjoyed by the monarchs of the glens, ran, 'The King's in London and it's a far cry to Loch Awe.'

The Myth of Granny's Heilan' Hame

I suppose we should blame the kailyard school of Scottish writing – the exponents of gushy rural sentimentality – from around the turn of the twentieth century for the fact that, when director Arthur Freed visited Scotland in 1953 looking for a suitable Highland village to film *Brigadoon*, he returned to Hollywood frustrated. He could find nowhere that even resembled the couthy, phoney, romanticised version of rural Scotland which the Americans wanted and, having read the literature, clearly believed existed. You know the sort of thing – the hump-backed bridge, the rustic shepherd and his bleating flock, the smoke curling up frae the but and bens and Dr Finlay doing his rounds. It's a terrifying thought that, half a century on, American visitors are still looking for that mysterious village which lies somewhere between a house with green shutters and a kailyard.

Digging up the Natives

Before the Second World War, famed novelist George Orwell congratu-
lated a correspondent for describing the Scots as 'Scotchmen' and not
'Scotsmen'. He declared, 'I find this a good, easy way to annoy them.' If
asked, most folk would guess that the term 'Scotch' is one which should
be exclusively applied to our national drink. Not so. Up until 1918, when
the name of the Scotch Education was changed to 'Scottish', it was
common usage to describe a whole range of Scottish entities, from the
Flying Scotchman to the Scotch fiddle. A stronghold of the old usage
remains in the Caledonian colonies in the United States.

An Absence of Backhanders

The idea that large-scale bribery was used to ensure the
passage of the 1707 Treaty of Union with England is now
widely discredited. Much of the £20,000 which found its
way north was related to pensions, arrears and debts and
more than half the total went to the Queen's Commissioner for expenses. Mind you, one individual who did
okay from the settlement was the messenger who
galloped south with the approved Treaty to London. He
received what, for the time, was the impressive sum of
£60. Now then, if we weren't bribed, were we drunk or
sleeping or not paying attention or insane or what?

Was Time on our Side?

There may be a rather stunning explanation for the epoch-making
Scottish victory over the might of England at Bannockburn in 1314 – it
was all down to timing. One nineteenth-century source suggests that, as
early as 1310, Robert Bruce was the proud owner of a Rolex watch, or at
the very least a clanky fourteenth-century equivalent, and he may have
organised his tactics to a strict timetable. Official recognition of the
invention of the watch did not come until 1328 in Germany, but we
must remember that the Bruce was very keen on his European
connections and was regularly in touch with the Continent. So who
knows?

The Years Fly By

Scotland's first alarm clock is thought to have arrived by ship at Burntisland in Fife in the 1500s – the product of piracy. Time, however, must have remained a kind of meaningless concept for most folk in Scotland for centuries after this if the story of the vanishing badger is anything to go by. Two friends – in 1800s Banffshire, if I recall correctly – were riding past a steep bank and pulled up their horses opposite a neat hole excavated in the slope.

'John, I saw a brock gang in there,' says one of the riders.

'Did ye, by God,' responds John, 'haud my horse and ah'll grip him.' Off speeds the bold John to the farmhouse along the road and returns with a spade before setting to work on the hole.

After half-an-hour's hard digging and 'nigh speechless' after his exertions, he reports, 'Ah, Dougal, ah canna' find him.'

Says his cool companion, 'Deed. I wad hae been stunned if ye had found 'im, John – it's ten year since ah saw him gang in!'

To Set your Watch By

On 7 July 1788, the London Mail pulled up for the first time outside the Saracen's Head Inn in Glasgow's Gallowgate – still a popular howff today. For over 60 years the horse-drawn mail service was so regular that shopkeepers in the East End of Glasgow set their watches by it.

Ahead of the Game

The use of the word 'parliament' to describe an important representative meeting for the consideration of matters of state first appears in the Scottish annals in 1173, some 70 years before it occurs in the English records – so there!

A Cultural Changing-Room

There is a story behind the naming of every Scottish pub that often reflects the nature of the community in which it is situated. My home town of Clydebank, for example, boasted among its plethora of public houses the 'murder mile' of the Dumbarton/Glasgow Road – The Cunard, The Seven Seas, The Vanguard and, up Kilbowie Hill, at a slightly more mystical level, The Atlantis, all betraying the town's shipbuilding heritage and its connection with the sea. However, my nomination for the most unusual must be Tigh An Truish, or the House of the Trousers, on Seil Island south of Oban. Here, islanders who wore a kilt out in the sticks in defiance of the post-Culloden legislation could change into troosers before catching the ferry for the mainland.

Two Lumps, Please

In 1906, *Forward*, a pioneering socialist journal and brainchild of Tom Johnston who was later to become the wartime Secretary of State for Scotland, was founded among the clink of teacups in the douce surroundings of Miss Cranston's Tearooms in Glasgow's Sauchiehall Street.

Honouring the Butcher

You'll often hear it said that St Andrews is the most Anglicised of the Scottish universities, with Edinburgh running a close second. But is there any firm evidence of this beyond the accents? Well, just a bittie. Did you know, for example, that, after the '45 uprising, St Andrews elected as Chancellor the infamous government commander at Culloden – William Augustus, Duke of Cumberland.

Hell on Earth?

In the earliest world maps – the famous Mappa Mundi – which normally show the earth as a disc, Jerusalem would be at the centre, paradise would be located near Sri Lanka, and clinging to the edge diametrically opposite paradise was Scotland. Of course, those early cartographers had never seen the Cuillins on a clear summer's evening.

Part of the Manufactured Scotland?

Gaeldom's annual gathering, The Mod – now well into its second century – has produced many popular singers such as Calum Kennedy and Anne Lorne Gillies. As you might expect, there are many Mod-ish anecdotes, including the tale of the legendary vanished Glasgow choir who were so enchanted by the scenery in Sutherland that they never went home. Nevertheless, the Mod is no 1,000-year-old festival rooted in the mists of a Celtic past. It was 'invented' in the nineteenth century during the surge of tartan mania laid at the door of Sir Walter Scott and 'Ossian' Macpherson, and stole the style of four-part singing from the Welsh.

Is God a Gael?

Get the dander up of a Gael on the subject of the antiquity of Gaelic (said to be the oldest written language in Europe, after Greek and Roman) and he or she will tell you that their language was also the language of the Garden of Eden – the tongue in which Adam and Eve whispered sweet nothings in each other's lugs. However, it was the eminent Gaelic poet, the late Iain Crichton Smith, who asked the big question, 'Does that mean that God spoke Gaelic as well?'

The Sough o' Hame

The great Scottish people in exile – emigrants and Scots descendants from Vancouver to Victoria State, from Auckland to Alberquerque – like nothing better than to celebrate what they perceive as their Scottishness. However, the expatriates have their critics. One speaker at a New Zealand Burns Supper, observed that 'The Scots have a deep abiding love of their country. They sing about it, write poems about it and after a few drams might even greet over it. They'll do everything but damned well stay in the place.' Billy Connolly, as usual, captured the essence of this idea when he cited the Scottish boomerang – it only sings about coming back! Already in the twenty-first century, however, a drift back to Scotland, which may yet grow to a flood, has been reported in some studies. Much will depend, I imagine, on the performance of our new parliament over the next few years.

The Blues and the Green

It's an interesting fact that a stretch of ground beside the Clyde at Glasgow Green called Flesher's Haugh, where the good Catholic boy, Bonnie Prince Charlie, reviewed his troops during the '45 uprising, was also the venue in the following century for Glasgow Rangers' first game.

So Many Scotlands

For many Scots, the thought that their roots are in Ireland is a difficult, uncomfortable concept. The fact is that, right up until the ninth century, there were people in the north of Ireland still known as Scots, the name given by the Romans and roughly translating as 'pirates'. The general view, held by historians and archaeologists, is that the Scots had started to arrive in Argyll as early as the fifth or sixth century. Another indisputable fact, which speaks volumes about the inevitable affinity of those early Gaelic peoples, is that, at the closest points, Scotland and Ireland are separated by only 14,000 yards of water – the sea bridge between the Celtic peoples.

Testing Times Ahead

Right up until the late 1700s, it wasn't only the English who regarded the Highlanders as the lowest of the low. Encouraged by the monarchy, Lowland Scots treated their Gaelic-speaking countrymen of the west and north as second-class citizens and, according to the historian T C Smout, usually referred to them as the 'Irish'. The ethnic mix of Scotland, of course, has been influenced by Gaels, Picts, Norsemen, Anglo-Saxons, Britons and Normans, among others. The idea of Scotland being a multitude of little Scotlands, overlapping each other in culture, religion, class and language is currently the favoured overview of scholars, writers and poets. Strength in diversity is the key phrase on everyone's lips. Can we live up to this proud boast? In a few years we should ask the East European asylum-seekers. But, for the moment, the answer would have to be maybe aye, maybe naw!

CHAPTER 12
The Greybeards Dun Good?

Religion, the Arts, Education and the Law

Neil's Brass Neck

After the victory of the Highland army at the Battle of Prestonpans in 1745, a message was sent to the ministers of Edinburgh in the name of 'Charles, Prince Regent' desiring that they should preach as normal on the Sabbath, which was the following day. Many of the clergy were alarmed at the stunning defeat of General Cope and his government army and fled into the countryside. Not much public worship took place in the city as a result, except at the Tron. At St Cuthbert's the minister, the Rev. Neil M'Vicar, preached to a large congregation, many of whom were Highlanders armed to the teeth. Neil prayed for King George II and also – after a fashion – for Bonnie Prince Charlie. His prayer was 'Bless the king, thou knowest what king I mean. May the crown sit long upon his head. As for that young man who has come along to seek an earthly crown, we beseech thee to take him to thyself and give him a "crown of glory".' When the Prince heard of M'Vicar's audacity, he is said to have laughed heartily.

Chain of Office

In the north-east of Scotland, where many of the earliest burghs were established in the Middle Ages, folk take a special pride in their towns and traditions. During a discussion on the relative merits of two north-east towns, one man proudly declared, 'We've got oor Provost and he wears a chain.' Totally unabashed, the other said, 'Oh aye, we hae a Provost tae but we let him gang aboot lowse.'

Taking Things Too Far?

King James III was reportedly so devout that he burst into tears every time he looked upon a representation of Christ or the Virgin Mary.

Creepy Crawlers

One of the oddest political gatherings of sixteenth-century Scotland was unquestionably the so-called 'Creeping Parliament' of 1571, assembled by the Regent in Edinburgh's Canongate. Under fire from the Catholic guns high above them on the castle rock, the members had to go about their business for much of the time on their hands and knees.

Five Miles of Torture

Papal legate Aenius Piccolomini, later Pope Pius II, was shipwrecked near Dunbar in 1435. As a mark of thanksgiving he decided to make the journey to the Marian shrine at Whitekirk on his hands and knees. Sadly, although he completed the five-mile crawl, he caught a chill from which it is said he never fully recovered.

Wee Charlie

Charles I, born at Dunfermline in Fife in the year 1600, was so sickly and weak as a child that, until his seventh year, he had to crawl around on his hands and knees. As a result of childhood rickets, he stood only five feet tall as an adult.

Let's Get Serious

When, after the staggering failure of Scottish nerve in the 1979 referendum, it was learned that a Welsh nationalist was threatening to starve himself to death to obtain a Welsh TV channel, the tongue-in-cheek Scottish response was that, to get an Assembly in Edinburgh, two Gaelic intellectuals were prepared to drink themselves to death.

Golgotha up the High Street

Eccentric and patriotic journalist Comyns Beaumont tried to rewrite the history books – and the bible – in the 1940s with a detailed theory which suggested that most classical and biblical sites were located in the United Kingdom. Most startling was his argument that Jerusalem was, in fact, Edinburgh and that Christ made his journey to crucifixion along the High Street.

Dark Side of the Law

The sinister-sounding Black Acts of Scotland were not magical rituals for king-making or calling down curses on our English cousins. They were simply the Acts of the Scottish Parliament up to 1587, which were reproduced in strongly emphasised black characters.

Justice (Roughly)

When we throw up our hands in horror at the seemingly barbaric sentences of mutilation and decapitation still handed out in some developing countries, we shouldn't forget that it isn't so many years since Scotland's legal system allowed what now seem to be totally inappropriate sentences to be delivered. In 1787, Thomas Gentles was hanged at Glasgow. His offence was stealing a piece of cloth from a bleachfield. Well into the 1700s, Highland chieftains conducted their own courts at which they were prosecutor, judge and jury – and occasionally, if we're to believe tradition, executioner too. At Gordonstoun in Morayshire, Sir Robert Gordon would throw transgressors into his bottle dungeon for the most petty of offences. One poor woman was cast into the pit for having rescued a cod's head from the laird's midden because she thought it might cure gout.

Mungo's Rough Start

Princess Thenew, mother of Glasgow's patron saint Mungo or Kentigern, is supposed to have crossed the dangerous waters of the Forth Estuary in a coracle while heavily pregnant, after being thrown out of the fortified settlement on Traprain Law, East Lothian. On reaching Culross after a storm-battered crossing, she promptly – and perhaps not surprisingly – gave birth to the future saint.

Too Long Among the Sassenachs

John Knox, Haddington-born father of the Scottish Reformation, spent so much time among English Reformers on the continent that, on a visit to Edinburgh in 1558, he was taken for an Englishman.

The Gravity of the Situation

The basic principles of the operation of the natural world which have guided humankind for the past three centuries – Newtonian physics – were being taught in the universities of Glasgow and Aberdeen before Sir Isaac's own university of Cambridge accepted them.

Let the Brain Take the Strain

Cynics will tell you that university students these days often find it difficult to fit in classes, what with their crowded social and sporting calendars. 'Twas not always thus. In bygone centuries the work was everything. Josiah Chorley, a student at the University of Glasgow in 1671, wrote about how 'sweet and pleasant' life was there. He described a 16-hour day of studies, beginning at 5 a.m. with the early bell. Such was the thirst for knowledge during the Enlightenment that some students at the University of Edinburgh attended every class they could cram into the day – even those only vaguely connected with their course of study. Today most students find that three lectures weekly can lead to brain implosion.

Cheap at the Price

In the 1830s – with rental for chambers costing £1 annually – it was possible to get a year's university education for a fiver. Now, how far would that go in the beer bar these days?

Who Let the Dogs In?

Scottish universities were not always the sanctuaries of intellectual enterprise that they would like us to believe. Sometimes the real world arrived with a bang. In 1831, 'sweeps, itinerant orators, ballad-mongers and a host of vagabonds' disrupted a meeting of Glasgow University students to discuss 'The Triumph of Reform'. Sounds to me like a pretty standard debate night at the Union.

Let Them Eat Cake

In 1433, the Bishop of St Andrews, Henry Wardlaw, made one of his most impassioned speeches at a parliament in Perth. He was anxious about the increasingly luxurious way of life being adopted in Scotland by the merchant classes. As a result of his pleadings, an act was passed banning the consumption of pies and baked meat by anyone below the rank of baron. Yet Henry himself was a grumpy old prelate if he didn't get his weekly Forfar bridie.

Keep Taking the Tablets

The Archbishop of St Andrews was, according to popular rumour, cured of a serious illness in the mid 1500s by being hung upside down by his heels for a week and fed with the flesh of puppy dogs.

In at the Deep End

Unrepealed laws still in force on the Scottish statute books include the loss of the right hand for a third offence of shooting pigeons and a piece of legislation designed to curb promiscuous sex – or fornication, if you prefer – with the guilty party being 'thrice-douket' in the deepest and most foul pool of water to be found in the parish. You have been warned!

Somebody Knew Something

The only known Act of a Scottish Parliament passed on English soil was approved at Twesilhaugh in Northumberland just before the Battle of Flodden in 1513. It dispensed with the usual feudal death duties of those who might be slain in the battle. This, of course, turned out to be one of the most chillingly timely pieces of legislation on the statute books because most of Scotland's nobility, including King James IV, perished in the battle.

Alice, the Mad Hatter and the Guinea Pigs

Had it not been for the children of Scots novelist George MacDonald – a man himself much given to the notion of mystical and fairy kingdoms – the world might never have seen Lewis Carroll's classic, *Alice's Adven-*

tures in Wonderland. Carroll read the story in draft form to the MacDonald children, who immediately approved. They have the thanks of youngsters who still enjoy a good read rather than the electronic massaging of the eyeballs.

The Gutter Press, Forsooth

Executions are macabre enough events but, over the years, untoward happenings have been reported even on the very threshhold of eternity. In 1863, according to Scots legal eagle Neil Gow, Mary Timney, a Dumfries mother of four, was condemned to death for the murder of a neighbour. Just as the bolt was to be drawn, a letter was handed to the prison governor. A reprieve? No, just a London newspaper looking for an account of the execution. And they say the present-day press corps is insensitive?

Earache and the Last of the Rotten Tomatoes

Isn't democracy, and in particular freedom of speech, a marvellous part of our everyday life and one which, just occasionally, we tend to take rather for granted? As MSPs deliberate, debate and legislate in the centre of Edinburgh, they would be as well to remember when they get over-critical of the administration that, as recently as 1689, William Mitchell was ordered to have 'his lug nailed upon the Tron' and was to stand there for an hour and face public ridicule for 'speaking agin' the government.

Punishment for all sorts of offences in the following century continued to stress the element of humiliation. For example, in 1725, convicted thief Margaret Gibbon was drummed through the streets of the capital wearing a false face and festooned with bells. In 1834, a Kelso woman was placed in the stocks for stealing clothes from a hedge where they were drying. A big crowd watched her humiliation and it's thought that this was possibly the last instance in Scotland of such a punishment. Politically incorrect it may be but an hour in the stocks with trousers round their ankles and lumps of sharn, rotten eggs and torrents of contempt being lobbed at them by passing schoolgirls might cure Scotland's more indisciplined youth of their bigsy attitude.

Fair Do's, Guvnor!

Here's a strange twist. When English justice was established at Leith under Cromwell's occupying forces in 1650, amazement was expressed at how the English justices were generally more lenient towards the Scotsthan the Scots had been to each other.

And One for Luck

In bygone years, Scots schoolchildren would complete their laborious repetition of the alphabet by adding 'eppershand' – effectively, the twenty-seventh letter. This was a corruption of 'and per se' or the ampersand, '&'.

A Breath of Fresh Air 1

The noted Scots chemist Joseph Black, born in Bordeaux, the son of an expatriate wine merchant, stunned his tutors at Edinburgh University when, in an extension to his thesis for his degree of MD, he announced his discovery of carbon dioxide. One commentator observed, 'There is perhaps no other instance of a graduation thesis so weighted with significance and novelty.' Something there for all final-year students to aim at.

The Heavy Mob in Early Modern Scottish Life

This would surely be a worthwhile dissertation topic for any student of our culture and heritage. As far back as 1606, the Privy Council banned parties in lawsuits arriving at court backed by a team of friends and supporters 'with a view to exerting an undue influence over the court'. Apparently, appearing mob-handed at court was custom and practice. The difficulties in enforcing such an order can be seen by simply visiting any sheriff court in the land today. Last year, a two-week random body-check of defendants, witnesses and hingers-on at Edinburgh Sheriff Court produced a haul of dozens of cut-throat razors, a five-inch gutting knife and a selection of hunting knives. This prompted calls, very understandably, for body armour for security staff.

Keeping his Feet on the Ground

The poet Lord Byron (1788–1824), who regarded himself as half-Scottish (his mother was Catherine Gordon, heiress of the Gordons of Gight, near Fyvie in Aberdeenshire), was known during his period of education at Aberdeen Grammar School as 'Wee Geordie Gordon'. According to one of his biographers, Geordie went on to Harrow and Trinity College, Cambridge, where he started writing some pretty abysmal poetry and perpetrated 'not a few follies'. Once he got his scanning right, things improved immensely.

A Gentle Chastisement for the Sun King

Louis XIV of France, a merciless and bloody persecutor of the Protestant faith, had an unusual toast which was to 'The Good Scotch Parson'. This originated when the king heard, through diplomatic sources, that the minister of the Barony Church in Glasgow, in the first years of the eighteenth century, prayed that the Lord should 'tak' the naughty tyrant of France [Louis] and 'shak' him o'er the mooth o' hell – but Lord dinna drap him in'.

A Breath o' Fresh Air 11

Scottish politicians are only occasionally guilty of cutting directly to the chase and abandoning the expected circumlocution, decorum and tact. Glasgow council leader Charles Gordon wrote a brief reply to his counterpart in a London borough during a dispute between the councils a few years ago thus, 'Away and bile yer heid! Yours sincerely . . .' C'mon Charlie, don't mince yer words.

Dark Ages Suicide Mission

The martyrdom of the monk Blathnac on Iona by Viking raiders in 825 AD is just one episode in a bloody period of Scottish history when Norse pirates ruled the waves and terrorised islands up and down the Scottish coast. There is one rather unusual aspect to the death of this particular monk. He was cut to pieces by the Norsemen when he refused to reveal the whereabouts of St Columba's shrine. However, according to the church chroniclers, Blathnac was an Irish aristo-crat/warrior-turned-monk, who settled on Iona after raiding began, with the specific intention of finding martyrdom at the hands of the boys from the longboats. They duly obliged.

Alasdair Gets the Boot

Among those who greeted Bonnie Prince Charlie, on his arrival in Scotland at the start of the 1745 uprising, was the Gaelic poet and Ardnamurchan schoolteacher Alasdair Macmhaigstir Alasdair. His employers, at the Scottish Society for the Propagation of Christian Knowledge which ran the school, didn't see his patriotism in a favourable light and sacked him. The SSPCK have been identified by historians as one of the agencies which strove to marginalise Gaelic and establish English as the language of social progress.

Nae Luck for the Bidie-in

Among the laws of Kenneth MacAlpine, the ninth-century king who unified the Picts and Scots, were some interesting statutes relating to marital responsibility. Allowance was made for wives committing criminal acts in the presence of their husband, who was to carry the sole burden of responsibility. Not so, however, for a concubine – who was held 100 per cent responsible for her own actions.

Keeping Sunday Sacred

Healthy sporting activity was fine with the old greybeards of the kirk in the aftermath of the Reformation – provided it didn't take place on a Sunday. In 1592, John Pitscottie and his naughty pals admitted that, on a fast Sunday at preaching time, they had been playing football at Muir-ton, Perth – ironically, many centuries later the stomping ground of the local senior football team, St Johnstone. The boys were ordered to make repentance but I'm prepared to bet it didn't halt their footballing activities.

There were apparently problems inside the churches too. Kirk records indicate that one of the jobs of the session officer in 1616 was to use his infamous red staff during services to 'wauken sleepers and remove greetin' bairns furth o' the Kirk'. These days I suspect the church would be glad of a few more greetin' bairns and, as for sleeping through the sermon, that doesn't happen any more, does it?

The kirk was clearly a lively sort of place in many ways. In the 1700s, dogfights at Sunday services were so common that kirks employed a 'nipper' armed with long-handled forceps to pinch the legs, tails and ears of the mangy curs who scrapped in the kirk precincts.

Taking to the Streets

In a remarkable demonstration of student–teacher solidarity, all the male pupils walked out of their class-rooms at Moffat Academy in February 1917 over the dismissal of the headteacher, Mr Ritchie. The boys paraded through the town carrying improvised banners made with sticks and tied with handerkerchiefs and, as they went, the battle cry was 'Ritchie Or Nobody'. It seems Mr Ritchie had been posted as a lieutenant to the Scottish Rifles and, as a result the school board decided to look for a successor. It restores your faith in the pupil–teacher relationship, does it not?

Sign Below, PLEASE!

One of the most stunning instances of over-optimism in Scottish history must relate to the first Protestant Covenant of 1557. This document, signed by five noblemen – the so-called Lords of the Congregation – had acres of space below the text for signatures. They never materialised as most people watched and waited to see if the Reformation was a mere passing fancy.

Pass the Nosegay Sharpish

According to the eminent Professor G W S Barrow of the University of Edinburgh, medieval Scotland was, quite literally, a stinking country. He describes the warm, homely smells of cattle, horses and hay and of food cooking in stone ovens or on open hearths mingling unavoidably with the acrid reek of peat fires; and the putrid odour of rotting meat or fish, or of untreated skins and hides. In addition, in every inhabited locality, the stench of human and animal waste would have been over-powering. But we should always remember that we are peering into the past from the intellectual high ground of the twenty-first century. It is conceivable that people loved their home turf despite the fact that it honked a touch.

Money Talks

The great medieval Scots historian Hector Boece (Boyce, if you're struggling), first principal of the University of Aberdeen, was a proud Dundonian, born there in 1465. He gave the town by the Tay the name 'Deidonum', broadly translating from the Latin as 'Gift of God'. As far as we know, he was not shortsighted. Famed for his imaginative *History of Scotland*, he was an old pal of Bishop Elphinstone, founder of King's College, Aberdeen, who wanted Hector as the college's first principal. However, Boece was reluctant to quit the learned society of Paris where he shared debates and drams with the likes of the philosopher Erasmus. Money finally talked, the clincher being an annual salary of £2 3s 4d. Suggestions that the deal included a season ticket for Pittodrie and free beer in the Student Union are, however, thought fanciful.

Smart Kids – Don't You Just Hate 'Em?

Historian Thomas Macaulay, born of a Scots family in Leicestershire, was an infant prodigy who read constantly and, as a wee tot, developed an amazing vocabulary. He was described as the greatest blether of his generation and started to write a compendium of universal history at the age of seven.

At a more regal level, when ten-year-old Alexander III, King of Scots, was married at York to Margaret, daughter of Henry III, in 1251, he refused Henry's request to do homage for Scotland, stating, with a wisdom and diplomacy way beyond his years, that it was too important a matter to debate at a wedding feast – a shrewd advisor or a wee guy of ten going on 50? It's anybody's guess.

Compassion Conspicious by its Absence

In the 1700s, breakaway groups from the Church of Scotland called Seceders or Dissenters threatened to undermine the whole establishment of the Kirk. There was no love lost between the 'rebels' and the Church. One Lanarkshire minister concluded a prayer condemning a dissenter thus: 'Oh Lord, Thou knowest that the silly, snivelling body is not worthy to keep a door in Thy house. Thresh him, oh Lord, and dinna' spare; oh, thresh him tightly with the flail o' thy wrath and make a strae wisp o' him tae stap up the mooth o' Hell!' Love thy neighbour as thy self – aye, that'll be right.

When the Saint Goes Missing

The only naturally occurring snake in Scotland, so I'm told, is the viper. St Patrick, said to have been born at Old Kilpatrick in Dunbartonshire (near the old bus station), rid Ireland of its snakes but where was Paddy when we needed him here?

The Old Dead Dog Trick

On the first Sunday after the Disruption in the Church of Scotland in 1843, when the Free Church broke away from the established Kirk, the change was registered in bizarre ways across the county of Sutherland. In Durness the church bell was muffled with an old sock, while at Farr a dead dog was hung over the pulpit.

A Hard Citizen

Robert Macqueen, Lord Braxfield, Lord Justice Clerk of Scotland in the 1790s, was a man who liked a drink and hated the radicals in equal measure. He is seen by the legal fraternity as having been a talented judge but someone who played fast and loose with judicial procedure. During a political trial, he remarked to one of the jury as he headed for the jury box, 'Come awa', Maister Horner, come awa' and help us hang ane of thae damned scoundrels.' Also, when it was pointed out to him by one of the witnesses that Christ himself had been a reformer, Braxfield chortled and replied, 'Muckle he made o' that – *he* was hanget.'

Too Much, Too Soon

Alexander Stuart, natural son of King James IV, was still a teenager when he was killed at the Battle of Flodden in 1513. Astonishingly, he had been appointed Archbishop of St Andrews – senior cleric in Scotland – at the tender age of 15.

Don't Blame the Proddy Mob This Time

The chief agent of destruction for Scottish churches during the early, angry years of the Reformation in the mid 1500s was not, as is widely trumpeted, the Protestant rabble but simple neglect by the faltering, corrupt Catholic Church. Failure to keep church roofs in good repair saw numerous buildings become ruinous just as the first stirrings of the new faith began to be felt.

The University of Perth

It was ironic that James I should have been such a fan of the city of Perth. At one point, in the early 1400s, he gave serious consideration to moving Scotland's only university at St Andrews to the town by the Tay. However, it was in the Fair City that James met his end, murdered in 1437, ventilated by a wheen of dagger thrusts at the Dominican Priory by a group of dissident nobles.

Literacy Is the Business

The Education Act of 1872 is often held up as the watershed when reading and writing became available to all. However, in Scotland it seems that we were already well on the way to that target. By 1871, more than four-fifths of Scots males and over three-quarters of women signed the marriage register rather than simply making their mark. Not proof of reading ability, of course, but circumstantial evidence of a highly literate population. The impressive impact of the Scots on earlier European education is also well illustrated by the fact that, between its founding in the early medieval period and the Reformation, the University of Paris had at least 17 Scots rectors.

Pushing her Luck

The fifteenth-century chronicler Walter Bower tried to show the risks in taking the name of the Lord in vain. He described how a group of young girls, returning from the foreshore at Rosyth after scavenging for shellfish, were caught in an electrical storm. As the lightning flashed, all but one of the girls crossed themselves. The rebel among the group merely shouted, 'Christ's cross upon my hinder end.' You've guessed it. She suffered an instant incineration, surely giving rise to the old Scottish declamation, 'Aye, yer erse on fire!'

CHAPTER 13

The Wandering – and Wandered – Scot

O'er the Hills an' Round the Bend

All Aboard the *Pudsey Dawson*

The emigration ships, which, over two centuries, took hundreds of thousands of Scots to new lives overseas, had some majestic and memorable names, such as *The Bengal Merchant*, *The British Empire* and *The Duchess of Argyll*. However, family records show that two of the most popular were those with the homely names of *Sea Gull* and my own favourite *Pudsey Dawson*. *The African Queen*, the scruffy little river puffer which starred with Humphrey Bogart in the award-winning film of the same name, was originally called *Livingstone* after the Scots missionary/explorer.

Walking Back to Wanganui

Remember walking, the art of pedal locomotion, the strange business of putting one foot after another in a forward motion – almost a lost art for most folk? Our Scots ancestors knew a thing or two about walking. Thomas Scott from Largo in Fife, a nineteenth-century emigrant to New Zealand, is, without argument, one of Scotland's greatest pedestrians. He was the long-distance postman on the Wanganui coast of North Island in the 1840s. His normal twice-monthly postal round covered 432 miles from Wellington and back. A non-swimmer and non-rider, Tam forded 11 rivers en route on a makeshift raft.

A man who matched this stamina was surely John Stewart, from Dually near Dunkeld, who, in the late 1700s, when already in his 80s, is reported to have walked from Perth to London in four days and six hours for a bet.

Something Fishy Here

During negotiations in the 1890s between Canada and the United States over the 49th parallel, it's reported that the Governor General of Canada, Lord Aberdeen, was persuaded that Oregon wasn't worth having because, unlike their Scottish counterparts, salmon in the Oregon rivers such as the Columbia did not rise well to the bait.

Changing Camps

In the sometimes baffling allegiances of the American War of Independence, Allan MacDonald of Kingsburgh – husband of Flora, saviour of Bonnie Prince Charlie – fought as an officer in the army of King Geordie against the patriots after emigrating in 1774. Returning to Scotland, the couple were blessed with five sons and two daughters. Many staunch Jacobites ended up supporting the British cause in America because of the chilling memories of the post-Culloden 'cleansing' of the Highlands and the fact that many had been forced to take oaths of allegiance to the king.

Fifers Forged Pittsburgh

The naming of the famous Pennsylvania steel town of Pittsburgh is attributed to General John Forbes of Dunfermline, who originally titled it Fort Pitt after seizing it from the French in the mid-1700s. By a remarkable coincidence, Andrew Carnegie, the steel multi-millionaire and philanthropist and Pittsburg's most well-known citizen, also came from Dunfermline.

The Big Tartan Apple

Generally the Scots in the United States did not band together in their own communities although, in the mid eighteeth century, we hear of a 'Scotch Quarter' in New York. However, this actually stretched along the Upper West Side of Manhattan Island.

A Wee Misunderstanding Immortalised

The quaintly named Kicking Horse Pass, one of the most important routes through the Rocky Mountains of North America, was named in the 1850s to commemorate an incident when Edinburgh geologist and explorer, Sir James Hector, parted company with his steed. The nearby river also carries the name.

Wherever You Lay Your Hat

Each year thousands of Arctic terns – tiny little birds with wings so delicate they are almost transparent – complete a remarkable 20,000-mile round-trip between the South Atlantic and the north of Scotland to breed. They undertake this epic flight to the same tuft of grass along the Scottish coasts where their antecedents have hatched for countless centuries.

In the human arena, it is reckoned that, between the end of the Napoleonic Wars in 1815 and the outbreak of the Great War, two million Scots emigrated, mainly to North America. A surprisingly large number of those, historians have discovered, actually came home again – perhaps over 30 per cent. And the Scots were on the road early as migrants, compared with many European nationals. In 1624, the citizens of Danzig on the Baltic were apparently dismayed by a steady immigration of 'miserable, debauched and weakly' Scots. By the mid 1600s there are thought to have been up to 40,000 Scots in the Baltic region and not all by any means were down on their luck. Many successful Scots traders and merchants and their employees operated in the area and were sufficiently well-off to support their own community churches and schools.

Of Stronger Stuff

The famous physicist Lord Kelvin entered the University of Glasgow at the age of ten years and four months. At the age of 14, Thomas Carlyle, possibly Scotland's greatest historian (even though he left his Scottishness behind him at Ecclefechan), walked 100 miles to enrol at the University of Edinburgh. Scottish students these days regard the two-minute hike from lecture to lecture as a trek of epic proportions.

Mincing up the High Street

In a bizarre attempt to end civil unrest resulting from feuds among his noble lords, King James VI ordered bitter foes to trot hand-in-hand in pairs from Holyrood up the Royal Mile in June 1587. The peacemaker's weird efforts to calm his troublesome aristocracy are said to have had a lasting effect – about 20 minutes, according to best estimates.

Hardly the Language of Eden

So many West Highlanders, many of them from the defeated Culloden clans, emigrated to North Carolina in the 1700s that even in the mid 1800s the business of the state legislature there was published in Gaelic as well as English. In addition, many of the slaves of these Highland settlers came to speak only Gaelic, making tracing their owners easier in the event of a slave escape. Professor Allan Macinnes, of the University of Aberdeen, observes that 'Gaelic became a brand of slavery'.

A Rootin', Tootin' Fire Chief

The tragic events in New York, on 11 September 2001, gave a new, heroic status to the job of firefighter. But the Scottish connection with this noble calling in North America stretches back to the earlier days of settlement. Fire chief McRobie, a Scots descendant and the boss of the Winnipeg 'smoke eaters' in the 1880s, is described as a colourful character who – after one particularly serious and dangerous blaze – rode his horse into the bar of the Canadian city's Queen's Hotel and ordered a whisky for himself – and, of course, a beer for his drouthy cuddy.

The Coffin Ships

It is known that ships used principally in the early nineteenth century to transport 'cleared' emigrants across the Atlantic were occasionally rotting, rusty hulks, known ominously as 'coffin' ships. Death was common on the Atlantic crossing, particularly among children, and one commentator told the whole story when he observed that the way in which Highlanders were crammed below decks would not be accept-able in the slave trade.

Kings Among the Grass Skirts

John Clunies Ross, a seaman who spent most of his life in the East and became known as the 'king' of the Cocos Isles, was born at Weisdale Voe in Shetland, the son of a schoolteacher, while Orcadian sea captain Daniel Ritch from Rackwick was crowned king of an island in the Fiji group and, among his thousands of subjects, were many who secretly practised cannibalism. A remarkable and exotic North Isles double.

The Other Side of Slavery

Perthshire girl Helen Gloag, after being captured and sold into slavery in the 1770s while on her way to a new life in the American colonies, eventually became Empress of Morocco.

The 'Ah Kent his Faither' Syndrome

In the sixteenth century, despite being a mongrel nation – a blend of Scottish, Pictish, Norse, Norman and Anglo-Saxon blood – the Scots adventurers all across Europe seem to have taken a special pride in nationality and also in kinship. In France, this pride in family is seen in the traditional put-down for boastful individuals, 'That man's a cousin of the King of Scots.'

With Aching Heart

After months of planning, the last of the line – hereditary piper to the Clan MacLeod, John Dubh MacCrimmon – was ready, in 1795, to emigrate to America. However, on the pier at Greenock, as his ship was prepared for sailing, the emotional scenes of departure and the thought of leaving his homeland, possibly for ever, were just too much for John. He picked up his bag and headed back to Skye.

Families in the Western Highlands and Islands, cleared from the land of their ancestors to make way for sheep, often took a handful of soil from the family grave on the long sea voyages to Canada or Australia.

Bring Forth the Tartan

Senator Trent Lott, the man who, in the 1990s, piloted the bill that made Tartan Day – a US celebration of all things Scottish – an official event, is also the man who made history by being the first person to wear the kilt on the floor of the US Senate. The tartan was Buchanan.

Eye of the Beholder

Angus McAskill, the 'Cape Breton Giant', was born in Berneray, off Uist, in 1825 and emigrated with his family to Canada at the age of six. He grew to 7 feet 9 inches and weighed 30 stones.His greatest feat of strength was to lift a ship's anchor weighing 2700 lb in New Orleans.

The men from the Highlands and Islands weren't always giants. A French general – like his emperor Bonaparte – was said to have been very conscious of his small stature but declared, after several campaigns against the Highlanders, that he was reconciled to his size, having witnessed the wonders performed by the 'little Scottish mountaineers'.

The Yukon's All Yours

Glasgow-born John A Macdonald, first Prime Minister of Canada, was responsible not only for the straight lines which divide Canada into provinces but also for setting up the Canadian North West Mounted Police – the world-famed Mounties. Its first commander was another Canadian-Scot, James F MacLeod, who was given 300 men to keep the peace in a territory the same size as mainland Europe.

Impression of Another World

The first images of Australia, after the establishment of the penal colony in New South Wales in 1788, were produced by a Dumfries landscape artist called Thomas Watling who had been transported with the First Fleet for forging Bank of Scotland guinea notes. In his journals, Watling complains endlessly about the way in which convicts were treated worse than the local Aborigine tribes. With the general view among administrators and officers that the Aborigines were sub-human, it does suggest that prisoners had a status problem.

Muir's Observations

It is the transported Glasgow radical lawyer Thomas Muir (1765–99) whose poetry first described the Australian backwoods. In one piece, he describes the Aboriginal hunting technique of torching the forest to flush out animals – 'from bush to bush with rapid steps he flies, till the whole forest blazes to the skies'. It's clear the twenty-first-century Australian bushfires have a long pedigree.

The Great Hopping Beast

Scots botanist Sidney Parkinson, who worked out of London's celebrated Kew Gardens and was famed for his plant sketches, joined the first expedition with Captain Cook to the South Seas in the 1760s. He is credited with producing the first-ever drawing of a kangaroo. It's said, incidentally, that, while Parkinson was sketching, Cook's crewmen asked the Aborigines for the name of the strange, pouched hopping creature. They were told 'kangaroo'. The sailors went away happy but it later transpired that 'kangaroo' was the local Aboriginal dialect phrase for 'Sorry, old bean, I don't understand a word you're saying.'

Pic Men Par Excellence

William Carrick, a pioneer of Russian photography whose descendants still live in Russia, was born in Edinburgh in 1827. Scotland can also claim a little-known pioneer of photo-journalism. Paisley-born Alex Gardner emigrated to the United States and, in New York, in partnership with Matthew Brady, he was the first person to take photographs specifically for newspapers. Perhaps his most notable work came during the American Civil War, with his battlefield scenes and his portraits of Abraham Lincoln that are still seen throughout the world.

Oh, Flower of Scotland

The thistle, according to tradition, was adopted as the symbol of Scotland after a Viking raider, treading barefoot for stealth at the Battle of Luncarty in Perthshire in 990 AD, tramped on a clump of them and let out a yell, alerting the slumbering Scots and signalling a famous victory.

The Thistle Transported

When Scots pioneers reached New Zealand in 1840, they were already making plans for their first St Andrew's Day celebrations, which included the ceremonial planting of specially imported thistle seeds. Across in Australia the thistle was also introduced by homesick Scots and, by the 1850s, it had flourished in Victoria to such an extent that it was declared a pest. In Queensland, settler George McKay from Thurso sent the council men packing when they arrived to cut down his 'Scotch thistle' which had been spreading like wildfire on his farm near Boonah. Seeing his national emblem put to the scythe was more than old Geordie could stand.

After You, I Insist!

Thistle tea was used in yesteryear as a cure for depression and Highland weans would eat the inside of the bulbous head of thistle, which is said to be sweet and chewy.

Warm Spells Predicted

Lanark-born William Lithgow, adventurer and travel writer whose peregrinations (published in the early 1600s) are regarded as the first genuine travel book written by a Scot, was once imprisoned and tortured by the hot-metal merchants of the Spanish Inquisition on the Costa del Sol.

On the Road

Records show that, in the fourteenth century, there were three main groups who regularly applied for passports to go to England – pilgrims (seeking spiritual aid), scholars (seeking knowledge) and merchants (seeking to make a quick buck).

Storming Those Old Male Bastions

A Kelso-born lass Jenny Trout, who emigrated as a child to Ontario in Upper Canada in the mid 1800s, is recognised as the first Canadian woman to be licensed to practise medicine. When she decided to study, no medical school in Canada would accept a woman so she enrolled and graduated across the US border in Pennsylvania.

Keeping up that Scottish tradition of breaking down the barriers of male prejudice in the land of the maple leaf was Bertha Wilson, from Kirkcaldy, who, in 1982, was the first woman appointed as a judge in the Supreme Court of Canada.

Black Berets, Striped Simmets at the Ready

French naturalisation was granted to the entire Scots nation by Louis XII in 1513 when the Auld Alliance was at its warmest. Despite various manoeuvres by the London parliament after Union, the order has never been officially repealed by the body which really matters, a bona fide Scots parliament. Of course, the Scots reciprocated and gave the French similar privileges in the time of Mary Queen of Scots but, since then, the French have had bigger fish to fry and you'll struggle to find anyone in France who gives a pain au chocolat for La Vieille Alliance.

Home of the Big Cheese

The Scots influence in Canada is extensive. For example, the town of Perth, Ontario, famed principally for having created the world's biggest cheese (6 feet high by 28 feet in the round), is located, as you might hope, on the River Tay but – confusingly for native Scots at least – is the seat of Lanark County.

Children of Botany Bay

Scottish female convicts were in great demand in the early 1800s in the Australian penal colony of Port Jackson, Sydney. To increase the female population, 1,500 Scots women, with their children, were shipped Down Under over the years at the request of the local administration. Among the women, there seems to have been a mixture of responses to banishment. One young Scottish girl is said to have died of a broken heart before the ship left the Thames, while another spoke of transportation as a blessing because in Scotland it was as if 'the plague were upon us'; they were hated and shunned wherever they went.

These Scots ladies included: Margaret Brown, a woman of many aliases, vagrant and fortune-teller (banished, 1793); Janet Cattenach, a Braemar thief, transported for seven years; Janet Hislop, transported for seven years for assisting an escapee; and Margaret Scott, prostitute and thief, transported from Perth in 1833. The vast majority of women were sent to Australia for offences of theft. Seven years transportation was the sentence for Glasgow weaver William Cuthbertson in 1839. His crime – radical agitation, attempted murder? No sir! Willie stole a pocket handkerchief.

Fashions in Geneology

Many Australian Scots can trace their ancestry back to the Botany Bay residents and such a heritage – a source of embarrassment for much of the twentieth century – has, with the dramatic increase in interest in 'roots' and genealogy generally, become almost cool in recent years, particularly if you can find a political radical in your lineage. Proportionately, far fewer Scots found their way to the Australian penal settlements principally because the Scots penal code never had as many capital offences (transportation was seen as an alternative to execution) as the English system and simple banishment was a common Scottish punishment. Mitigating circumstances played an important role in Scotland and only modest punishment was imposed for theft – until the third offence when things began to get heavy. Only 97 Scots were executed in the 20 years before the establishment of the Australian colony in 1788, while there were 890 executions in London and Middlesex in the same period from a population about half the size.

The Water Magician

Fochabers boy John Thomson was an inventor of great resourcefulness and imagination, who emigrated with his family to New York State in 1854. His greatest of several claims to fame was the installation of 20,000,000 of his patent water meters in homes and businesses throughout the United States.

Batty Over the Big Apple

Fans of the caped crusader, please note. Washington Irving, son of an Orcadian merchant who emigrated to America in the 1700s, is credited with giving New York its nickname of Gotham City. Irving – America's first great man of letters and the first American to earn his living as a writer – is also considered to be the originator of the short story form.

The Man in the Barrel

Hideaways have an interesting pedigree in Scottish history. Glasgow-born Allan Pinkerton, a cooper to trade and founder of the famous American detective agency, honed his skills as a private eye by hiding inside barrels and listening to criminal conversations.

In Safe Keeping

For security reasons, Scotland's most precious historical and antiquarian documents – including the Declaration of Arbroath, the Articles of Union and Mary Queen of Scots' letters – were housed, for five years during the Second World War, in the basement of the Sheriff Court at Oban. One of the great Scottish historians of the twentieth century, Gordon Donaldson, was given custody of the Great Seal of Scotland for the duration of the war and was so serious about his job as temporary keeper of this national treasure that he slept with it under his pillow.

Beneath the Drifts

Epic snowstorms in Scotland's north-east have, on occasion, completely buried houses – and occupants. Once, according to Buchan legend, rescuers trudging through a blizzard arrived late-on at a buried croft to find only the chimney poking up above the drifts. Their calls down the lum were answered by the elderly occupant. The rescuers then shouted reassuringly, 'We'll hae ye oot in a meenit, Alex.' Came the response from the depths, 'And what wid ah be wantin' to be oot on a filthy nicht like this!'

The Emptying of St Kilda

The little-known 'first' evacuation of St Kilda – the lonely island group way out in the Atlantic, west of the Hebrides – took place in 1852 when 36 people, a third of the population, set out on the sailing ship *Priscilla* for Victoria, Australia, seeking a better life. Because of fever on board, only 16 reached Melbourne alive. The final evacuation of the islands came in 1930 and the windswept archipelago was bequeathed to the National Trust by the Bute family. It is now a magnet for ornithologists, archaeologists, anthropologists and devotees of wild, abandoned locations.

First-Footing Canada

One version of the Norse discovery of Canada (Vinland) in 1010 by Thorfinn Karlsevini suggests that two Scots were among his crew. More certain is the origin of the first map of the St Lawrence River published in 1542. It was drawn by Jean Rotz who, we're told, was the son of David Ross, a Scots merchant who had settled in Dieppe.

A Plummy Accent, Forsooth

Sir John Clerk of Penicuik, who sent his son to Eton in 1715, is given the doubtful credit for starting a trend among the Scots nobility which has created, some say, a remote anglicised aristocracy, speaking the accents of the cultured south. 'That's surely a bit oaf,' I hear our gentry complain. Yet Sir John was only following a creeping anglicisation which goes back centuries. In his Statutes of Iona in 1609, James VI showed his determination to civilise the 'barbarian' Highlanders and obliterate the heathen 'Irish' language by insisting that every laird who owned 60 or more kye should send their eldest son for education in the Lowlands.

Down a Peg or Two

A Texas rancher who was visiting some friends in Carse of Stirling was making great play on the relatively small size of the average Scottish farm.

'Back in Texas,' he boasted, 'it takes me a full day to drive to the edge of my property.'

Said his Scots host, 'Aye, ah used tae hae a car like that!'

INDEX

Index

Index